26-03 BK Bud

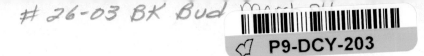

P9-DCY-203

How to
Find Hidden
Real Estate
Bargains

SOUTHEASTERN COMMUNITY
COLLEGE LIBRARY
WHITEVILLE, NC 28472

How to Find Hidden Real Estate Bargains

Robert Irwin

SOUTHEASTERN COMMUNITY
COLLEGE LIBRARY
WHITEVILLE, NC 28472

HD
1382.5
.I73
2003

Second Edition

McGraw-Hill

New York   Chicago   San Francisco   Lisbon   London
Madrid   Mexico City   Milan   New Delhi
San Juan   Seoul   Singapore
Sydney   Toronto

The **McGraw·Hill** Companies

Copyright © 2003, 1991, 1986 by The McGraw-Hill Companies, Inc. All rights reserved. Printed in the United States of America. Except as permitted under the United States Copyright Act of 1976, no part of this publication may be reproduced or distributed in any form or by any means, or stored in a data base or retrieval system, without the prior written permission of the publisher.

3 4 5 6 7 8 9 0   DOC/DOC   0 9 8 7 6 5 4 3

ISBN 0-07-138876-1

This book contains the author's opinions. Some material in this book may be affected by changes in market conditions, changes in real estate law (or in interpretations of the law), or changes in the way bidding on properties is handled, since the manuscript was prepared. The accuracy and completeness of the information contained in this book cannot be guaranteed. Neither the author nor the publisher is engaged in rendering investment, legal, tax accounting, or other similar professional services. If these services are required, the reader should obtain them from a professional.

 This book is printed on recycled, acid-free paper containing a minimum of 50% recycled, de-inked fiber.

McGraw-Hill books are available at special quantity discounts to use as premiums and sales promotions, or for use in corporate training programs. For more information, please write to the Director of Special Sales, Professional Publishing, McGraw-Hill, Two Penn Plaza, New York, NY 10121-2298. Or contact your local bookstore.

Contents

Preface

This is the third writing of this book. The first edition was written in 1986, a period of, then, unparalleled growth in real estate. That book began with the sentence, "Are there still any real estate bargains out there?" Few people thought there were.

The first edition was revised in 1991, when real estate prices were falling across the country, when homes were so overbuilt they were auctioned off, when no one would buy for fear that prices would go lower in the near future. Given this down market, again few people thought bargains really existed.

This new edition finds prices soaring once more. And yet, people again question whether they can still find real estate bargains.

The one constant of each edition (witness the sustained demand for this book over more than two decades) is that it affirmatively answers the question, "Do real estate bargains really exist?"

Of course, the real estate bargains of 1986 or 1991 are no longer out there. They are long gone. However, there are many new bargains today, along with new ways of financing and negotiating for them.

This book is especially intended for those who have expressed an interest in seeing an updated version on bargain hunting in real estate. It has been rewritten for a new century and a new market. And, as you'll see, it includes many, many bargain-hunting opportunities.

Robert Irwin

1

What Is a Bargain in Real Estate?

I have a good friend who says he never pays retail for anything, including real estate. Now it's easy to understand how he could get bargains on clothing, tools, even cars, because discount prices are advertised everywhere. But how does he get a bargain price on real estate? That's what you're going to learn in this book.

Real estate bargains are everywhere, but you have to know where to look and what to look for. Some homebuyers, for example, feel that getting 5 percent off the asking price when purchasing a house to live in is a real bargain. And for them it is. On the other hand, some investors don't feel it's a bargain unless they can get 50 percent off the market value of the property.

If you're going to profit big in real estate, you're going to have to think more like those investors and less like those homebuyers.

On the other hand, it's not always a matter of getting a big discount on price. There are other kinds of real estate bargains. For example, you might be happy to pay full price for a property if you could get a mortgage carried back by the seller at half the going interest rate. That could be a real steal. Or perhaps you'd be thrilled by a seller carrying back a mortgage with no payments at all for 3 years, dramatically improving your cashflow. As we'll see, bargains come in lots of different shapes and types.

But I'm sure many readers are wondering about the big question: Are there truly real estate bargains out there? Can you really purchase a home with a market value of $200,000 for $150,000? $100,000? Or less? Can you actually get spectacular financing?

Yes you can, but don't take my word for it. Go through the chapters of this book. Read about foreclosure auctions, HUD and VA repos, Marshals sales, GSA and IRS auctions, bank and private individual REOs, and much more. You'll quickly come to realize that the hidden secret of real estate is that there are far more bargains out there than most people real-ize. Indeed they exist in every area of the country.

But you may be saying to yourself, it takes money to make money. Don't I need a lot of cash to take advantage of these bargains?

Yes, sometimes. And sometimes not. Often, a lot depends on how clever you are with financing. And in other situations it depends on how creative you can be in your negotiations with the seller. Yes, money does talk, but it's not the only speaker in town.

You too can find hidden real estate bargains if you know where to look and how to negotiate.

2

How to Get Started Bargain Hunting

When I wrote the first edition of this book in 1985, I began with the question: Are there still any real estate bargains out there?

Now, looking back from the perspective of almost 20 years and a new century, how I wish I had bought more property back then! Indeed, compared with prices today, 1985 seems like the happy hunting ground of real estate bargains. If you bought *any* property back then, chances are it would be worth far, far more today.

The same applies today looking to the future. Although prices seem high to us, ask yourself what they will be like 20 years from now. If you answer, as I think most people will, that they will be far more expensive, then you've answered that first question. Indeed, real estate bargains are everywhere.

This doesn't mean that some properties aren't more of a bargain than others. The goal of this book is to help you find those properties that are underpriced even in today's "high-priced" market.

Bargains Can Be Anywhere

I can recall showing a large old house on an R-2 lot (zoned for two dwellings on the property) to an investor I hoped would buy it with me. When we got out of the car, he walked around the house and commented that it was in run-down condition, the seller was asking too much considering the neighborhood, it wasn't in the world's best location, and the financing was terrible. In the short space of 5 minutes, he gave me several excellent reasons why he would never live in the "dump."

But, I pointed out, the lot was R-2. "R2, G2, who cares?" he said. "I'm not interested in investing in junk real estate. Show me a clean house in a good area and we'll talk."

Later that day I showed the same property to a different investor. She didn't even bother to look around it. All she wanted to know was whether it was zoned R-2. I said it was.

We bought the property, "split" the house (divided it, making it into two separate rentable units), and sold it as a duplex within a short time for a substantial profit.

Moral? The first investor didn't know a bargain when he saw one. The second did. There's no way you can find a bargain if you don't know what to look for.

The Three-Bedroom, Two-Bathroom Dream Bargain

Real estate bargains aren't limited to splits. There's everything from repos to tax auctions; from probates to discounted seconds; from "junk" locations to million-dollar "fixers." We'll look into all of these areas and more in this book, but first let's see how good you are at recognizing a bargain when you see it.

Would you recognize a bargain if you saw it? To help find out, try answering the following question. The way you answer reflects how you visualize what constitutes a bargain in the real estate market.

Question: What does a typical real estate bargain look like? No, it's not a trick question. But it is an important one.

I've asked this question to many people. Here's the most common answer I've received: "The typical real estate bargain is a three-bedroom, two-bathroom house that probably needs paint and minor repairs and is located in a fairly good neighborhood but is selling for way below market price."

Was your answer something similar? If so, it's perfectly understandable. This is a bargain that we *all* can recognize. A good home, a good neighborhood, a little fixing, and a low, low price. It's a sweet deal that anybody would take in a minute.

But that's the problem. If we have a good house that's in a good location and is easy to fix up, why should it sell for way below market price?

This is not to say it couldn't happen. Seller's distress (discussed in Chapter 21) might result in a lower price for an immediate sale. However, chances are that such a house will sell easily enough for market price or perhaps at slightly below market for a very quick sale.

Keep an Open Mind

My point is that if the only bargain you recognize is the dream home we've just discussed, you may be waiting a very long time. Even in a market where sellers are everywhere, buyers are few, and prices are falling, choice properties will bring choice prices. *Compared with other houses,* the ideal "three plus two" will seem high in any market.

On the other hand, if you're willing to take a more open-minded approach—if you're willing to look at bargains in the form of terms offered by sellers, properties that need fixing up, or any piece of real estate that you can make a profit on—then you could very likely find a suitable bargain this very week.

Develop a Style

This is not to say that you will always be looking for bargains in a wide variety of types of real estate. Most successful bargain hunters develop a "style." They find a particular type of property that they can easily understand and work, and then they specifically hunt for it.

However, until you know what your own style is, keep an open mind. Be prepared to look at all types of real estate. Don't start excluding properties until you've made a thorough examination of what's out there and the benefits they offer you.

"I Wouldn't Live in That!"

Finally, don't try to find bargain property based on where you would or would not live. (There are two important exceptions to this that we'll explore later in the book.) It could be a one-room shack or a fifteen-room mansion, a pizza parlor or a six-unit building. Whatever it is, it's an investment—and probably not your first choice for a personal residence.

If you're buying stock, you don't judge the company on the basis of whether or not you would live in the home office. If you're buying commodities, you don't judge your purchase on the basis of whether you personally drink orange juice or eat soybeans. Similarly, if you're buying bargain real estate, don't judge it on the basis of whether or not you personally would live in it. Rather, look at it in the cold light of profit or loss. Your motivation should be: Can I make money on this property? If you can, consider it. If not, dump it.

Locating Bargain Areas

Now let's move on to locations. Where are the bargain locations, those areas that have special bargain properties, whether in an up or a down market?

As we'll see, any area at all can have bargain properties. However, we are frequently looking not only for bargains but for affordable bargains. We want to find something that we have the money to handle. For some of us that may mean bidding on very expensive properties, but for most of us bargain hunting involves looking for less expensive real estate. Nevertheless, chances are that your ideal piece of property is located nearby.

Finding Cheap Properties in Expensive Areas

This is a matter of matching your pocketbook to what's out there. You may be able to afford a $50,000 house that's for sale in Phoenix. But what if you live in Los Angeles, where in many suburbs the minimum price is over $300,000? If you want cheaper real estate, how do you find it?

The answer is that, almost without exception, cheaper (or more expensive) property is nearby regardless of where we live. If you look, you can almost surely find a cheaper (or more expensive) area in which to hunt. If you don't believe this, try the following experiment.

Buy Close to Home

Get a map of your local area and a drawing compass. Put one end of the compass on your home's location on the map and extend the compass so that it draws a circle with a 50-mile radius (if your map's scale is 1 inch for 10 miles, then open the compass to 5 inches). Anything within that circle is probably not much more than an hour away and is a suitable bargain hunting territory for you. Forget anything outside the circle.

It would be a rare area of the country indeed that did not have a wide variety of property located within a circle with a 25-mile radius. (We are, after all, talking over 1000 square miles.) Even if your residence is located within an area of expensive property, somewhere in some direction no more than 25 miles out you're likely to find an area with much less expensive property. The opposite also works: You can usually find a much more expensive area than yours within the circle.

Once you've found an area that feels comfortable, stake it out. Get to know it. Farm it. Claim it as yours. If you're going to find bargains there, you'd better know that area better than anyone else does.

I always try to buy real estate that is as close to my home as possible. The reason is that I can be nearby if there are any maintenance or management problems. In any event, the property should be no farther than I can comfortably drive within a half hour or so. (The exception here is that you may know of an excellent property manager in a distant location.) I therefore estimate that what I buy should be no more than about 25 miles from my home.

What about the Competition?

Some bargain hunters are overwhelmed by the thought of competition. "There must be dozens, hundreds, thousands of other bargain hunters out there. They may be more experienced than I am. They may be brokers and attorneys. What chance do I have?"

My standard reply is, "Damn the competition—full speed ahead!" In real estate I've found that the best way to handle the competition is to ignore it. This is particularly effective because in most cases the competition is mainly in our minds.

Yes, other brokers and investors will indeed be in competition with you, but not all of them at the same time. Once you limit your location and discover the type of property you want (your style), you'll find that you've eliminated 90 percent of your competition. As for the 10 percent that remains, not all of them will be actively looking on the same day you are. Some will already have found bargains and will be out of the market. Some won't have the cash or financial resources available when the bargain appears. And others won't be looking at the same spot you happen to be when you discover your bargain.

Don't Underestimate Inertia

Never underestimate the power of inertia. Few of us really put forth the energy to get us off dead center. While you're out there actually looking, chances are that 99 percent of your remaining competition is sitting home thinking about looking.

When you find your bargains, you will often discover that you're all alone, with nobody else around at the moment competing with you. I've often found that to be the case.

You don't want to hesitate because bargains are like honey. Just as honey attracts bees and flies, bargains will eventually attract other investors and treasure hunters. You have to be ready to act immediately.

Get a Game Plan

Finally, you need a plan. In many respects this is the single most important asset a bargain hunter can have.

Do you need a game plan to win at real estate bargains? Think of it this way. The Patriots or the Rams or some other top pro football team comes to the stadium for the Super Bowl. Before the game they huddle around the coach, who says to them, "Let's get out there and win!"

The players give a cheer. Then, as they run out onto the field, one of the tight ends asks the quarterback, "What are we going to do? What's our game plan?" The quarterback shrugs his shoulders and says, "I don't know. We'll just pass the ball around a bit and see what happens."

Sure they will, and at the end of the game, they'll be down by 40 points. In order to win, football teams have a strategy that they follow. Usually, the team with the best plan wins.

Bargain Game Plans

It's the same in business and particularly in real estate. It's not enough just to look for and find bargains. You must have a plan for what to do once you've found the bargain.

A very successful bargain hunter I know never buys a piece of real estate, no matter how much of a bargain it seems to be, until he has a firm "escape plan" in mind. This is a plan for getting rid of the property and collecting his profits. Here are some typical game plans, or escape plans, for real estate bargains:

1. Immediately resell (flip) the property for a profit.
2. Hold it long term and rent it out for cashflow and/or tax benefits.
3. Refinance it to get your cash out; then hold or dump it.
4. Trade it for other property.

The game plan should be thought out well in advance of a purchase. For example, if your plan for a particular property is to resell it quickly, you should see to it that when you make your purchase the financing is easily assumed by the next buyer so that you will be able to get out quickly.

Or if your game plan is to hold it long term, you should see to it that the payments are sufficiently low that you won't have a negative cashflow. (As investors know, a negative cashflow means that your expenses exceed your income.)

The investor friend I mentioned advocates having at least two escape plans—one long term and one short term. Your short-term plan may be to resell quickly. But if for some reason that proves impossible, your long-term plan may involve holding and renting the property until you can sell it.

Find a Mentor

Many of the hidden bargains we'll discuss include foreclosed or seized properties. Although the purchase procedure is usually outlined in detail by the seller, not all of the consequences of the purchase may be obvious. The property could have a redemption period during which the former owner has the right to take the property back even after you've bought it. Perhaps there are hidden mortgages or other liens against the property. Or the condition may be much worse than you think.

All of this goes with the territory, and as you become an experienced bargain hunter, you'll know how to deal with it. Initially, however, it can be confusing and tricky. Therefore, my suggestion is that if you're just starting out, try to find a mentor, someone who's been through it before and can pave the way for you.

Mentors include other investors, real estate agents, attorneys who specialize in bargain properties, and even people who work for the various sellers. It could be almost anyone who is knowledgeable about the workings of the market in your area and is willing to take you under his or her wing. Look for such a person.

TIP

Attend foreclosure seminars. These are held across the country by various lenders and public agencies. Their purpose is to help people who are threatened by foreclosure understand the process and their rights. You can sometimes meet people in foreclosure who want to sell their properties, so this is a potential source of business for you. However, you can also meet others like yourself who are investors and who can potentially become mentors.

As I'm sure you're aware, we've only scratched the surface on finding hidden bargains. But that, after all, is the topic of this book. In the next chapters, we'll explain how to find specific bargains, such as foreclosures, repos, or fixers.

3

Bargains in Foreclosure

Mention real estate bargains and the first thought that usually comes to mind is foreclosure. If there's a bargain to be found, most people assume that this is where it is.

Foreclosures do, indeed, offer opportunities for bargain hunters. Here it is possible to obtain properties for a fraction of their market value.

For example, let's say you've found a neighborhood where the average house sells for about $150,000. Being a bargain hunter, you're looking for a highly motivated seller, one you can lowball and perhaps, in exchange for a quick sale, negotiate a price of 10 to 15 percent under market.

But as you walk the neighborhood, you notice a house that seems abandoned. The doors are locked, the windows are boarded up, and the lawn has turned to weeds. You stop by a neighbor's home, which is well kept, and learn that the former owner of the decrepit home couldn't make the mortgage payments and the bank is foreclosing.

So you do some investigative work (we'll see how shortly) and discover that the house will be sold next week by the lender to the highest bidder "on the courthouse steps."

Of course, the lender will bid the full amount of the mortgage plus interest and costs, which you have learned comes to $75,000. But could you bid $75,000 plus $1 and get the property?

If you could do that, think of what a steal it would be. You'd be getting a property for virtually half of the market price. That's far better than any deal you are likely to negotiate with a lowball offer. Now that's a bargain!

Does It Really Happen?

Yes, foreclosures with enormous bargain potential do occur. They happen all over the country and in boom times as well as bust.

When the economy is down, as it was during the 1990s, the rate of fore-closure was much higher. In recent years, particularly during the boom of the early twenty-first century, foreclosure rates dropped. For a short time, prices were rising so rapidly and houses were selling so fast that it was eas-ier for people in foreclosure to sell their way out of the problem. Unless they were "upside-down," they could find a buyer to bail them out by pur-chasing the property and paying off the old loan.

TIP

Being upside-down means that the borrower owes more on the property than it's worth. This can easily happen with the no-down loans and up to 125 percent of value loans that have become popular. If the borrower gets into financial trouble and can't make the payments, there simply isn't enough equity in the property to be able to resell (particu-larly when you add in a real estate commission and sales costs).

More recently, foreclosure rates have returned to their usual levels of around 350,000 a year nationwide. (The actual number of borrowers who are somewhere in the foreclosure process—30 to 90 days delinquent on their mortgage—is estimated to be around a million or more.) In other words there's no shortage of foreclosed properties out there.

Are All Foreclosures Bargains?

No, not all. One of the hardest concepts to grasp for someone new to this field is that you're better off staying away from most foreclosures. They aren't a bargain; they're a trap.

To see why, let's go back to our example of the house with the $75,000 mortgage. We assumed that the *only* mortgage on the property was this one loan. But what if there were others?

For example, what if this was a second mortgage and there was a supe-rior first mortgage of another $75,000 ahead of it? Further, what if there was a tax lien on the property for another $10,000. Here's what the lien structure on the property could look like:

Tax lien	$ 10,000
First mortgage	75,000
Second mortgage	75,000
Total owed	$160,000

In this case the total owed against the property exceeds its market value. If the lender of the second mortgage were foreclosing and you were to pay $75,001, you'd end up owning a property that still had $84,999 in liens against it. You would have in effect lost $10,000 in the purchase process.

TIP

A *lien* is anything involving money that encumbers the title to a piece of property. A mortgage is a lien, a judgment is a lien, and taxes can be a lien. For practical purposes this means you have to know what liens are on the property before you can safely make an offer to purchase.

Remember, just because it's a foreclosure doesn't necessarily mean it's a bargain. As we'll see, there are many pitfalls between the success stories.

What Is the Foreclosure Process?

While the foreclosure process varies state by state, throughout the country the process is similar whether your state uses a trust deed or a mortgage. (See Chapter 11 for more information on the difference between the two.)

From the perspective of the bargain hunter, there are three separate times when you can buy the property during the foreclosure process. They are:

1. From the borrower when he or she is in default

2. From the trustee or court when the property is sold on the courthouse steps

3. From the lender who now owns it (called an REO)

In this chapter we're going to concentrate on number 1, which is before the auction. Number 2 will be discussed in Chapter 11 and number 3 in Chapter 4.

When the Borrower Is in Default

If a borrower doesn't make the payments on the mortgage, the lender's ultimate recourse is to take back the property. This can be a long or short legal process depending on your state. In states that use a trust deed, the process typically takes a little less than 4 months from the time the lender files the first "notice of default."

IMPORTANT NOTICE

IF YOUR PROPERTY IS IN FORECLOSURE BECAUSE YOU ARE BEHIND IN YOUR PAYMENTS, IT MAY BE SOLD WITHOUT ANY COURT ACTION, and you may .have legal right to bring your account in good standing by paying all of your past due payments plus permitted costs and expenses within three months from the date this notice of default was recorded. This amount is   Plus Estimated Fees and Expenses as of   , and will increase until your account becomes current. You may not have to pay the entire unpaid portion of your account, even though full payment was demanded, but you must pay the amount stated above.

However, you and your beneficiary or mortgagee may mutually agree in writing prior to the time the notice of sale is posted (which may not be earlier than the end of the three-month period stated above) to, among other things, (1) provide additional time in which to cure the default by transfer of the property or otherwise; (2) establish a schedule of payments in order to cure your default; or both (1) and (2).

After three months from the date of recordation of this document (which date of recordation appears hereon), unless the obligation being foreclosed upon or a Separate written agreement between you and your creditor permits a longer period, you have only the legal right to stop the Sale of your property by paying the entire amount demanded by your creditor.

To find out the amount you must pay, or to arrange for payment to stop the foreclosure, or if your property is in foreclosure for any other reason, contact:

YOU MAY LOSE LEGAL RIGHTS IF YOU DO NOT TAKE PROMPT ACTION.

If you have any questions, you should contact a lawyer or the government agency which may have insured the loan.

RECORDING REQUESTED BY

AND WHEN RECORDED MAIL TO

NAME
STREET
ADDRESS
CITY &
STATE

Att

REFERENCE NUMBER

In states that still use the older judicial foreclosure procedures (and mortgage as evidence of indebtedness), it can take anywhere from a few months to a year or more from the time the lender files a complaint (and records a *lis pendens,* or notice of legal action). And there is still the matter of an "equity of redemption," in which the seller or other lienholders may come back and reclaim title afterward by paying off the old mortgage, costs, and interest after the sale. (We'll have much more to say about this in later chapters.)

Nevertheless, it is possible, regardless of the type of instrument used, to purchase the property during the first stage, when the borrower is delinquent in payments and the foreclosure process has started but has not concluded. Let's take an example.

Terri is our owner. She bought her house a few years ago. The purchase price was $300,000. Here's how she paid for it:

Down payment	$ 15,000
First mortgage	285,000
Purchase price	$300,000

TRAP

Just 10 years ago a 90 percent loan to value (LTV) mortgage was uncommon. Today 95 percent, 100 percent, even 103 percent mortgages are made every day by lenders. Because of the low or no down payment and the higher mortgage amount, the chances of these borrowers not making payments and getting caught in foreclosure are increasing.

Terri made more than enough money at her job as an advertising executive to keep up the payments, which she dutifully did. However, after several years of ownership, she lost her job and had trouble finding another. (At the time the country was experiencing a recession, and jobs were difficult to come by.) Without income her meager savings were soon exhausted, and she found she couldn't keep making the mortgage payments. After 3 months the lender moved to foreclose on the property.

TIP

Lenders are in the business of making loans, not taking back property through foreclosure. Typically, they will allow a borrower ample opportunity to make good on missed payments. Most will try to institute some sort of a payback plan spread over a year or more. Rarely will a lender begin foreclosure until the borrower is at least 2 to 3 months in arrears.

As in most of the country, Terri had signed a trust deed. Because she was in California (the model many states use), the foreclosure process was relatively short. After filing a notice of default, the lender had to give her 90 days to make up all back payments and costs. If she did this, the mortgage would be reinstated and she could continue living in the house and making payments. (However, the lender would undoubtedly notify credit reporting bureaus that she had been in default, making it more difficult for her to secure credit in the immediate future.)

After the 90-day redemption period, the lender would need to advertise the property in a "legal" newspaper for 21 days. During this time Terri could no longer reinstate the loan by paying up all the back payments. She could, however, save her property by paying off the loan and all back interest and costs.

TIP

A "legal" newspaper is one that carries legal notices. Usually, every major city has one. You won't find it on the newsstand, but anyone in the courthouse will tell you where to buy a copy. Subscriptions are usually quite expensive, but if you're a serious bargain hunter, you'll want to consider subscribing. It will alert you to notices of *lis pendens* and notices of default as well as provide information about auction sales.

After the 21-day period, the property would be sold to the highest bidder on the courthouse steps (stage 2). After that the home is irrevocably lost to her. She has no further right to redeem it.

During all of this, Terri continued to occupy the property and the lender did little to bother her (short of sending threatening notices). This whole process was a nightmare for Terri. She wanted desperately to get out of it, to somehow sell her home, pay off the mortgage, and get a fresh start. That's where we come in.

We can contact Terri directly. Since she is going to lose her house if she doesn't act, and since she doesn't have the money to act, we can offer her several solutions:

1. We can offer to assume or pay off the existing loan including all back payments, interest, and costs *if* she is willing to deed the property to us. (Our costs will be 3 to 6 months' worth of mortgage interest plus the lender's costs.)

2. We can offer to do the foregoing plus give her some money for her equity (if she has any). The amount will depend on how big her equity is. (Our costs are going to be significantly higher, but ideally, they can be covered by a new mortgage.)

3. We can offer to do the foregoing plus allow her to stay in the property as a tenant so she won't have the trouble and expense of moving. (The danger here is that if Terri wasn't able to make the mortgage payments, chances are she won't be able to make the rent payments. As her landlord we'll have the responsibility of evicting her, which is sometimes a costly, aggravating, and time-consuming process.)

TIP

In all three cases, we don't need much cash. If we have credit, we can secure our own financing on the property that will pay off the existing loan and give us the additional funds necessary to make the deal.

Why Step in to Save the Borrower?

The reason is to get a bargain property. Terri wants out. We are willing to accomplish this for her *if* she is willing to give us a suitable bargain for our trouble. Remember, there are risks at each step of the game for us (which we'll go into shortly), and taking these risks can only be justified by suitable rewards.

The key to all of this is the market value of the property. Remember, Terri owes roughly $300,000. If the current market value is only $310,000, for example, there's not enough room here for us to make a profit. On the other hand, if the market value is $350,000 or $400,000, it suddenly all makes sense.

Why Wouldn't the Borrower
Save Herself?

Most borrowers who get into trouble make the attempt. (But not all. Some hide their heads in the sand and refuse to take any action that might help their situation. They prefer to falsely believe that foreclosure will never really happen.)

Seeing that she was in danger of losing her property, Terri may have made some effort to liquidate her house. Once she realized that she couldn't continue to stay there (if she in fact realized this), she probably put it up for sale and even listed it with a broker.

TRAP

Find out if the borrower has filed for bankruptcy. (Many facing foreclosure do.) If the borrower has filed, he or she may not be able to sell you the property without court approval. The borrower-seller may not know this or may forget to mention it when you're negotiating a preauction purchase.

If it's listed, it will complicate things for us. Now the broker will want a commission, typically 6 percent, or in this case around $18,000. That leaves both us and Terri less to work with.

However, Terri may have insisted the property be listed for so high a price that it doesn't sell. Perhaps the market is bad. Or her house may simply have fallen through the cracks.

For whatever reason, the listing simply may not have worked out. Now Terri may be trying to sell the property for sale by owner (FSBO). This is far more difficult because most buyers don't want to deal directly with sellers. (They prefer the cushion and security an agent offers.)

TIP

If you're going to be very successful at finding hidden bargains, you'd better learn to handle transactions yourself without an agent. Or be prepared to pay the agent's fee.

Assuming Terri is not currently working with an agent, we can present those options we've decided on (one, two, or three listed earlier) to her.

Will the Seller Take Our Offer?

The likelihood of that happening depends in large part on how close to actually losing the property she is and on how realistic she can be. Some people look at the matter logically and quickly come to an agreement. Others choose to moan and groan and pretend that the auction day will never come.

If Terri goes along with our offer and if we've drawn it carefully so that there's a reasonable profit built into it, we can take the property off her hands, perhaps give her some money for her equity, and most certainly help her avoid a foreclosure on her credit. Along the way, we will have obtained a bargain property.

What Can Go Wrong?

Buying a home in the preauction market has some serious perils. For one, there's the competition. As soon as someone gets behind in payments, they tend to check with mortgage brokers and loan officers to see what their options are. Word quickly gets out, and they are soon inundated with offers to refinance their property. Often, however, these are of little help because without a job, as in our example, it's difficult to secure new financing. Nevertheless, it's a hope that a borrower-seller has that may prevent him or her from acting in a timely matter to solve the problem realistically.

Also, once the lender begins foreclosure proceedings and notice is given to the public (as indicated earlier), other bargain seekers may write or call with essentially the same offer as you. Any savvy borrower-seller will begin pitting one against the other, and you could find yourself in a bidding war to help this person out of foreclosure.

TRAP

Beware of foreclosure bidding wars. Use a sharp pencil and know what your real costs are. Bidding tends to make the blood boil and to force the price up. The last thing you want is to pay too much for a property.

There are also offers from the Internet. I recently logged on to a fore-closure Web site as Albert Einstein (as a joke) to see what it offered. It didn't offer much. However, within half an hour, old Albert had 21 e-mails offering to buy his property out of foreclosure, sight unseen and without even knowing the lien structure or market value! True, most of these offers were probably nothing more than a scam. But misleading information such as this can keep a borrower-seller from acting in a timely manner.

What many times happens is the borrower-seller dithers too long, and suddenly, time is too short. The borrower-seller "suddenly" realizes that the lender is going to sell the house on the auction block in a few days. Now they come to you and want you to bail them out, right now!

You may feel moved to action. However, this is not a situation you want to enter into lightly. You need time to investigate the title. Remember, until you check you won't know if this is the only mortgage on the property or if there are others that may be in a superior position. And there may be tax or other liens as well. All of this could greatly reduce the seller's equity and seriously affect the price you're willing to pay.

Are There Any Laws to Watch Out For?

Finally, there's a relatively new body of law that protects sellers from the "foreclosure consultants" we become when we offer to purchase during the foreclosure process (between the time the notice of default or complaint is filed and the property is sold at auction). When we offer to buy during the foreclosure process, we may be putting ourselves in jeopardy with the law.

Some states may require us to give the seller 5 days to rescind our pur-chase agreement. Although this may not sound like a lot of time, if there are only 2 days until the auction, it puts us in a real bind.

Other states offer a redemption period to someone who sells to a fore-closure consultant during the foreclosure process. For example, we might buy the property only to realize that the seller has 6 months dur-ing which he or she can buy it back simply by returning our purchase price plus interest. That makes it very hard for us to resell or fix up the property.

Check with an attorney or good real estate agent who is familiar with the laws on foreclosure in your state. You don't want to fall into the trap of wasting your time, effort, and money only to have a tenuous hold on the property.

What about Assuming the Seller's Mortgage?

Thus far, we've been speaking as if the only method of buying out of foreclosure was to pay off the old mortgage by getting a new one. Indeed, as a practical matter, this is usually the case because of the alienation clause in almost all modern mortgages.

TIP

An *alienation clause* is one that says the mortgage becomes immediately due and payable upon transfer of title to the property. Also known as a *due on sale clause*, it keeps anyone from assuming the existing loan without the lender's permission.

We could give the borrower-seller enough money to redeem the defaulted mortgage (pay up the back payments, interest, and costs). Now the mortgage would be current. However, as soon as the lender learned we had transferred title from the borrower-seller to ourselves, it would again start foreclosure proceedings, this time not because the loan was in default but because the alienation clause had been breached. Thus, there is a need to come up with new financing.

TIP

Be sure to check the loan documents, which the borrower-seller should have, to see if the loan in question has an alienation clause. If it doesn't, buying the property suddenly becomes a whole lot simpler.

Some enterprising bargain seekers will endeavor to get around this alienation clause. Once the loan is fully reinstated, to begin foreclosure again, the lender must usually start at the beginning of the process. This means that once the lender finds out that you've bought the property and assumed the loan (or taken it "subject to," which means you don't assume responsibility for it), it could be anywhere from a few months to a year before the lender can take the property back through foreclosure. So, these bargain seekers hope to have a breathing space during which they can fix up the property and resell it.

Keep in mind that bargain seekers here are not doing anything illegal. Violating the alienation clause in a mortgage has a specific noncriminal penalty—foreclosure. They're just buying time. It usually takes a pretty gutsy person to do this. After all, the property might not fix up and/or sell quickly, and the lender could start breathing very close by. But then again, you can always refinance, or try to.

TIP

You can negotiate with lenders. Go talk to the lender. It may be willing to let you assume the existing nonassumable mortgage, or even give you a new and higher one, if you agree to pay the current interest rate.

TRAP

Some bargain seekers may try to circumvent an existing mortgage's alienation clause by *not* recording the deed. The idea is that what the lender doesn't know can't hurt you. Unfortunately, this is not the case. By not recording the deed, you leave yourself wide open. Remember, the order of recording determines ownership. Until you record the deed, the property is not "officially" yours. More liens can be recorded against the former borrower-seller, which is a real possibility given that most people in foreclosure have other financial difficulties. Further, the former borrower-seller can even go out and borrow on the property and can even sell it again! Not recording the deed is potentially the worst solution.

How Do I Find Properties in Foreclosure?

We've already suggested one method: Check the public notices in your area's legal paper. It is usually published at least weekly.

However, one problem with this is that the location of the property is often given as a legal description. For example, suppose you learn that a certain property is in the foreclosure process, and the location is given as:

> Lot 59 of Tract No. 1041 as per map recorded in Block 25 Page 46, in the office of the county Recorder, county of xxxx.

Unless you can translate this into a street address, it's not of much help.

To translate, you'll need to go to the recorder's office and look up the description, which will lead you to a map on which streets and addresses can be interpreted. Another alternative is to take it to a title insurance company, where for a fee (or free if you're friendly with one of the officers) it can be translated.

Perhaps a better solution is to check one of the foreclosure newsletters. These exist in any major and most smaller cities. Here someone has gone to the trouble of checking all of the foreclosure notices. They are republished and not only is the common street address given, but often the phone number of the borrower-seller and that of the lender (along with its address) may also be listed.

Someone has done the legwork for you. However, you'll have to pay for it. These newsletters frequently cost $100 or more a month in subscription fees.

Contact Title Companies

Yet another way to find out about foreclosures is to contact title insurance and trust companies, particularly the big ones. Often, they have records indicating who is in foreclosure.

Title companies have these lists because they are frequently a party to the foreclosure. For example, in states where a trust deed is used, the title to the property rests with a trustee. When the lender (the *beneficiary*) forecloses against the borrower (the *trustor*), the trustee puts the property up for sale. Guess who is typically named as a trustee? Right, it's the title and trust company.

Trustees are usually not individuals but trust corporations. They may be on the books as such for hundreds of thousands of mortgages. And of course, they know when someone is in default.

Some title insurance and trust companies will offer a list of their trustee actions to almost anyone who asks. (It is, after all, public knowledge.) Others are very proprietary and will only pass it out to "friends." The rule here is to try to know an officer in each of several big title and insurance and trust companies.

How do you get to know an officer? Become a client. As you invest, you'll be buying and selling a lot of property. Throw your business to a particular officer in a title insurance and trust company, and they'll be happy to help you in any way they can. Very quickly, you'll achieve client or "friend" status. Take them out to lunch once in a while. It could pay off with some very handy information.

What Do I Say to the Seller?

Okay, you've found a property in foreclosure. You like it. You knock on the door. Now what?

It can be awkward. It's kind of hard to pop in and say, "By the way, I understand you're losing your property. I want to buy it." But something that simple can work and produce positive results.

Remember, the borrower-seller is probably disgusted, angry, and perhaps more than a little frightened of the future. Anything that appears to promise a solution is likely to produce a positive reaction.

Besides, honesty is a great policy. Once you've found someone in foreclosure, don't hide the fact that you're in it to make a profit. We all want to know the other person's true motivation.

Emphasize that it can be a win-win situation. You can help them get out from under and possibly even salvage a few dollars at the same time that you make a profit. Just keep in mind that you may be the third person this morning who's made this pitch. Nevertheless, if you're sincere about helping, are reasonably well dressed, and appear ready and able to make a move, you'll get your audience.

Once you have the borrower-seller's attention, ask to see the mortgage documentation. Most people hang onto this, and chances are they'll have it handy now because of the situation they're in. (Sometimes the mortgage company will have helped by sending copies.)

Very quickly, try to determine how much the borrower-seller owes to cure the default on the mortgage. Subtract that from the value of the property (which you surely determined before showing up by getting a comparative market analysis from an agent, didn't you?). Keep in mind there could be other liens hidden that the seller doesn't disclose and which you'll need to research.

This establishes the seller's equity. Now subtract your profit and see if there's enough margin to make any kind of a deal possible.

It may be that the borrower-seller simply owes too much. If that's the case, then you'll have to make your apologies and bow out.

On the other hand, if there's sufficient equity, then determine your profit and, if there's still enough left, tell the borrower-seller how much you may be willing to give them, after you check out the condition of the title and other liens. The fact that it's anything at all should make them happy.

If their equity is too small to give them a payout, explain that by taking the property off their hands, you'll be saving their credit (or much of it). This will allow them to buy another home at some time in the future as well as get other loans and credit cards.

TIP

Sometimes borrower-sellers are afraid to say it, but they just don't have the money to move out. They could be completely broke. If that's the case, you may want to pop for their moving costs and, possibly, even the first month's rent at an apartment. Usually, this is only a grand or so, and it can have two important benefits. It can cement the deal. And it ensures that they'll be out when you get the property, so you won't have to worry about evicting them as tenants.

Many of us worry that we're poor salespeople and poor negotiators. But 90 percent of selling and negotiating is simply stating the obvious. (The other 10 percent is being scrupulously honest.) If the situation warrants it, you'll get your home. If it doesn't, there are plenty more to seek.

The Bottom Line

Check out the property. Check it out again. If it's a mess, figure out what's wrong and what it will cost to put it right (see Chapter 16 for more information).

Check out the title. Be sure you know who actually owns the property. (You don't want to get a deed from the borrower-seller's cousin who has no interest in the place and just happens to be staying there rent free when you walk in, but who'll sell to you for a case of Pepsi.)

Be sure you know what other mortgages and liens are on it. It might seem that the borrower-seller has a huge equity, until you discover that it's a third mortgage that's in foreclosure and there are even bigger second and first mortgages on the property.

TRAP

Typically, if there is more than one mortgage on the property, the first, which is usually the biggest, will foreclose first (because it has the biggest payments that can't be met). However, to protect its interest, as soon as the junior mortgage holder (second, third, or whatever) finds out, he, she, or it (if it's an institutional lender) will then make up the payments on the biggest (first) to get it out of foreclosure and then start their own foreclosure process. This protects their junior interest, and their mortgage usually allows them to add the costs of making the superior mortgage right, onto their loan. That's why it's not safe to assume that the lender doing the foreclosure is the only one, or even the biggest or first loan on the property. See the Appendix if you're not sure how the order of mortgages affects foreclosure.

Check out the amounts owed. Be sure you sharpen your pencil so you know exactly how much money is to be made (and if it's enough for you to take the risk) before you start.

Check out the laws pertaining to buying from a borrower-seller in fore-closure in your state. You don't want to do something illegal or anything that can cause you to lose the property later.

Check with an experienced attorney or real estate agent, particularly if this is your first time out. No, it's not hard. But it is tricky, and you want to be sure you do it right.

What about Numbers 2 and 3 for Buying a Property during Foreclosure?

Number 2 is buying at auction. As noted earlier, we'll explore this in detail in Chapter 11. Number 3 is buying after the auction from the lender. That's the subject of the next chapter.

4
Bargains in REOs

REOs are the most popular of the bargain opportunities in real estate. Here you might get a property for 5 to 50 percent off market value. Yet, they are usually considered a safer and easier way to buy real estate than purchasing either directly from the seller before a foreclosure auction (Chapter 3) or at the auction itself (Chapter 11).

Buying an REO means getting it right from the lender. You usually get clear title and perhaps even title insurance. You may get a property that's been refurbished. And as I said, if you're careful, you can get one that's way below market price.

By the way, *REO,* for those new to the field, stands for "real estate owned." It's actually a rather strange term because someone always owns real estate. However, it's particularly applicable here because it refers to lenders, such as banks, or large institutions, such as the Federal Housing Administration/Housing and Urban Development (FHA/HUD) or other organizations, owning real estate. For them this is a no-no because their purpose is to lend (or insure or guarantee the loaning of) money, not to own property. Having to take property through foreclosure indicates a failure of their lending policies. That's why real estate owned is such a good way of describing a bad thing for the lender but a good thing for you.

Why Don't Lenders Like REOs?

There are many reasons. REOs don't pay interest, and lenders are in the business of earning interest. Whenever lenders have money tied up that isn't producing interest, it shows up as a negative in their bookkeeping. (It's actually listed as a liability and not an asset.) Too many properties in the REO category can lead to insolvency in a lending institution, and that can lead to its failure. REOs simply don't look good on the books of a lending institution. As I said, they indicate failure rather than success. Finally,

REOs take time and effort away from the lender's main business, which is making money from loans.

For these and other reasons, lenders are always anxious to get rid of REOs as quickly as they can. However, no matter how fast they dispose of them, more crop up. During the real estate recession of the 1990s, their numbers increased dramatically. More recently, there have been fewer. But there are always plenty for the bargain hunter.

Are There Different Types of REOs?

Yes and no. Generically, the term means any property taken back through foreclosure and owned by a lender. However, properties owned by the federal government are frequently called government repos (although in this chapter we refer to the whole field as REOs). Those owned by private companies, such as banks, are strictly called REOs.

HUD may be the biggest owner and seller of REOs in the country, acquired through defaulting FHA mortgages. The Veterans Administration (VA) is also big on REOs acquired through defaulting VA loans. Other branches of government from the Small Business Administration (SBA) to the Marshals Service have REOs that they want to dispose of. We'll look into these and more in the next few chapters.

On the other hand, banks large and small make real estate loans that sometimes go bad. And when these are taken back, they are referred to as private REOs. And when an average citizen takes back through foreclosure a house that he or she sold with a second mortgage, these are sometimes called private individual's REOs (see Chapter 5 for more information on these).

In this chapter we focus on bank REOs. These are owned and offered for sale by banks and other similar lending institutions.

What Does a Typical Bank REO Look Like?

HighInterest Bank had an REO on its books. It was a three-bedroom, two-bathroom house in a fairly good area of town. HighInterest Bank was hoping in the worst way that it could get rid of that property. It wanted to convert it from a liability back into a mortgage that paid interest. In other words, it wanted someone to buy the property.

TIP

Banks could rent an REO and generate some income in that fashion. However, their expertise is in lending, not in property management. Besides, a rented house is harder to sell than a vacant one. As a result, they usually won't do this unless the market is so bad that they can't otherwise dispose of their REOs.

To get rid of the property quickly, the bank was willing to accept a price of 10 percent below market. (The market was $150,000, and the lender would accept $135,000.) In addition the bank was willing to give a buyer a 30-year fixed-rate loan for 2 percent below the market interest rate and that with only 5 percent down.

Is it a bargain? As indicated before and as we'll see in later chapters, it is possible in many situations to get a better price, better financing, or a lower down payment. But what makes this a bargain is that all three areas are offered at better than normal conditions. As an all-around bargain property, this REO is hard to beat.

Why Do Lenders Try to Keep Their REOs Secret?

If I've whetted your appetite for REOs, you'll have to hold in the reins for a bit. Sometimes there's a problem finding out about them. One would think that as anxious as lenders are to get rid of REOs, they would be out there advertising and promoting them, doing their darnedest to get investors to buy them. But that's not the case at all.

Although big banks have become more open about their REOs and frequently list them with agents on the multiple-listing service (MLS), small banks can be very secretive about their REOs. They would prefer that most people don't even know they exist. (And most people don't.) They have three good reasons for keeping REOs quiet.

First, banks are corporations. Like other corporations, they have stockholders. If the stockholders get wind of the fact that the lender has a large backlog of REOs, it's going to erode investor confidence. Some nervous stockholders are going to begin selling stock. When that happens, others may hear of it and a general stock panic could ensue. The stock values could plummet, and that would hurt the lender, particularly if it's a small local bank.

Second, banks depend on their depositors for their funds. Even though most lenders have federal deposit insurance up to $100,000 per account, depositors are finicky (particularly those who deposit more than $100,000). The rule seems to be: If I stick my money in a bank, I want to be sure the bank is in good shape even before I worry about the insurance.

If lenders acknowledged that they have a lot of REOs, it might shake depositors' confidence. If depositors started pulling out their deposits, it could start a catastrophic run on the bank. With a large bank, this is unlikely. But it could be a serious problem for a small bank.

Finally, announcing a lot of foreclosed property could adversely affect the real estate market. If buyers were aware of what's really out there in REOs, they might cut back on buying regular resales and new houses. This would hurt the lenders' opportunities for making new mortgages.

These are three very good reasons that banks, particularly small ones, would like most of us to overlook the REOs that are out there.

How Many Bank REOs Are There?

I don't know of any reliable figures for bank REOs, but the figure nation-wide is probably more than 100,000. Large banks have hundreds, sometimes thousands. Smaller banks, however, may only have a handful. However, it's with these smaller local banks, as we'll see, that real opportunities can abound.

The vast majority of bank REOs are houses and condos. Frequently, they are in fairly nice areas. A few are in the best areas . . . or the very worst.

Are All Bank REOs a Good Deal?

In many cases they are, although it really depends on what you're looking for. As we've noted, REOs usually combine a little of all the items we look for in bargains. They are a little below market, the terms are a little better, the down payment is usually a little less, their locations are usually at least adequate, and there are usually no occupancy problems. However, if you want a big price discount, unusually terrific terms, or nothing down, you probably won't find these here.

Bank REOs are often far better than average deals. Many are true bargains. But they usually aren't steals. If you're looking to "steal" a property, you'd best look elsewhere.

Are Small Bank REOs Better?

I've found this to be the case. With a large bank, there's usually an established REO office for each region of the state. They process many properties and go through them quickly. Frequently, they have agents lined up to handle the listings. In other words it's a production line, and it can be hard for you to break in and get individual attention.

With a local bank, however, there may be only half a dozen REOs a year. They are assigned to one of the bank's officers, who handles the properties on a part-time basis. This person often already has a full workload, and this is piled on top. If you can present this officer with a way to get rid of these REOs in a quick and economical fashion, he or she may jump at it. It's a fact that many small bank REOs are disposed of privately.

TIP

Don't think that there are only big banks around. Almost every community has a small local bank, or two or three. There are thousands of them across the country. The big banks dominate advertising, but the small banks are often highly profitable and have a few REOs they are dying to get rid of.

How Do I Find Out about Bank REOs?

That, of course, is the trick. With some lenders being so secretive about them, you won't find REOs waiting for you to come along. In fact the most difficult part about this area can be finding the properties.

The most logical first step is to check with a lender. Go into your local bank branch and ask for their REO department. As an experiment while writing this book, I tried that with five different banks. In four cases the people I talked with had no idea what I was talking about. In the fifth the person said that she knew and then connected me with their "real estate division." It turned out to be a subsidiary of the bank that was a residential real estate sales office. They didn't handle REOs at all. It's pretty hard to get information from the lender when the lender's own people don't know what's going on!

But they do know, or at least the manager of the branch does. However, the information isn't going to be given to you just because you walked in the front door off the street. You could, after all, be a reporter doing an exposé on how many REOs this particular bank has at the time. Or you could be a blabbermouth.

On the other hand, if you're a depositor (particularly if you have substantial funds deposited) or a stockholder, then the lender's people will feel obliged to talk with you. Typically with a large bank, they'll say that their REOs are all listed with local real estate agents. They may even give you the number of the agent.

What you want, however, with a big bank or small, is the name of the officer who handles REOs within the bank. (Rest assured, virtually every bank has an REO department or at least an REO officer.)

If you're a stockholder or depositor, you should try to locate the most senior bank employee and convince this person that you really are an investor looking to purchase an REO. You may be lucky. (If you aren't lucky, there are other avenues; we'll be looking at these in a few paragraphs.)

If you are a stockholder or depositor and have flexed your muscles to reach the REO department or have convinced a branch officer to give you the location or phone number, you may find yourself quite unwelcome once you arrive. You may be the very person the lender doesn't want to give the information to for the reasons indicated earlier. Therefore, when you call or show up, the REO officer could indicate the following:

1. No list of REOs is available or even exists.

2. No properties are currently being offered for resale to the public directly by the bank. Any that do crop up are listed with agents.

3. If you leave your name and number, should such a property appear, you will be contacted.

The real story is otherwise:

1. A list of all REOs the bank holds does exist and is available. It includes the addresses of the properties, their condition, the exact amount the bank has in them, and their priority for disposal. Even common sense

tells us that such a list has to exist if for no other reason than internal inventorying at the bank.

2. All properties held as REOs are currently being offered for resale. The bank does indeed have its own means of getting rid of them.

3. You'll be called back the next time the sun freezes over.

How Do I Make Real Contact?

When you are rebuffed by the REO officer, you know one thing for sure: You're at the right place. The real questions now become: How do you get the information you want from this person? How do you get to be part of the means of disposing of the properties that the bank has? How do you become a part of the solution for the bank? There are at least three answers here.

Contact the Lender's Agent

Remember, this information is often readily available. Explain to the agent that you are interested in REOs. You'll be shown what, if anything, is available. Keep in mind that the bank is going to try to get top dollar for these properties. It may even have fixed them up or not depending on the circumstances. However, the agent is interested in getting paid, and that isn't going to happen until and unless there's a sale. So prod the agent for information.

How much does the bank have in the property? How little will it take? What special financing terms will it offer?

If the agent senses that you are sincere and have the wherewithal to make the purchase, he or she will probably work with you. As I said, the agent wants to make a sale as badly as you want a good REO.

Appeal Directly to the REO Officer

If done correctly, this is your best chance of getting a good REO deal. Here's how to do it.

First, consider the position of the REO officer. On the one hand, he or she has all these properties to get rid of. On the other hand, the lender probably doesn't want to publicize the fact that the institution has a lot of REOs. Think how you can solve both of the REO officer's problems.

Begin by not asking to see the entire list of REOs. Chances are you're not going to see it anyway, so there's no point in riling up the REO officer.

Next, try the following statement or something like it: "I'm looking to buy an REO in the following price range [name a price range, such as $200,000 to $300,000] in the following area [name an area, such as between Denver and Colorado Streets, on the west side of town, or north of the boulevard in Tarzana]. Do you have any there?"

Consider what you've just not asked. You haven't asked if the bank has a lot of REOs. You haven't asked how many. You haven't asked to see where they are located.

What you have requested is a very little bit of information about a specific price range and specific area. The REO officer isn't going to get fired for telling you that. In fact, if the REO officer tells you, he or she won't be admitting they have a lot of REOs and won't be saying where they are. (This solves the problem regarding publicity.) On the other hand, the officer may be helping to get rid of some of those REOs on the lender's books. (This solves the other problem regarding disposal.)

If you're ever going to convince an REO officer, particularly from a small bank, to tell you about properties, ask for a specific price range in a specific location.

Typically, the REO officer will now say something like, "Yes, we have a couple of properties in the area you are looking at. Here are their addresses. Take a look and see what you think." (If it turns out that the bank really doesn't have any REOs in the area or price range you've indicated, try changing the area or price.)

You've just reached the next plateau in your REO search.

Find the Property Directly

This bypasses the REO department entirely, at least with regard to locating the properties. Remember that the foreclosure process involves advertising the sale of the property and then holding a public auction. At that public auction, a price is paid and a deed is given, which is then recorded. All of this is public information, and if you have the time, you can go to the hall of records and dig it up. But there's a better way.

As noted earlier, in nearly every major metropolitan area of the country today, there are publications that record these facts. Sometimes it's called *REO Service*, other times *Foreclosure Facts*, and so on. You can also buy a service that will give you much of the following information:

- The name of the lender who holds the property
- The property's address

- The amount paid for the property at the foreclosure sale
- The name of the previous owner
- The date of the auction/sale
- The original loan amount
- The year built
- The square footage
- The property taxes
- The assessed land evaluation and the assessed improvement evaluation

These information services aren't inexpensive. They can cost as much as $200 per month, but they will put you in instant touch with REO properties.

You can find out about these services from a variety of places. Ask a lender. Check for advertisements in legal or business papers. Check with agents. Look for ads in the yellow pages of phone books.

Once you have the locations of the properties, you can pick ones in the specific areas you're interested in and check them out. When you've identified several you like, you can then go to see the REO officer.

This time, however, you're coming in with live ammunition in your hand. You already know the property you're interested in. You only have to say, "I understand you own the property at such and such address. I want to make an offer. Let's talk business."

Negotiate Terms with the Lender

Once you've located the property, it's time to make the best deal with the lender. It's important to remember that everything is negotiable, depending.

It depends on how desperate the lender is to get rid of the particular property and how much money the lender has in it. (No lender wants to sell for less that the former mortgage amount plus back interest, penalties, and costs, but they will if pressed.)

If you've found a three-bedroom, two-bathroom dream house in a wonderful area, don't expect the lender to be very anxious to cut the price or terms. You may end up paying close to market price and getting close to market terms. The reason is that if you don't buy it today, it's such a desirable property that the REO officer will feel confident of selling it to another investor tomorrow.

On the other hand, if you're interested in the worst dog the lender has, you may get it at or way below market, and the lender may offer financing that's terrific (1 or 2 percent below market rate and even an assumable loan.) For those properties in between, you'll get something in between.

Depending on your situation, you can also slant the terms. For example, you may have very little cash. You may make an arrangement whereby you give the lender virtually nothing down in exchange for getting a loan at market rate. You may put down more cash (say, 20 percent) in exchange for a loan at way below the market rate. Or you may pay cash (or get your own other financing) in exchange for a very low price.

What about Fix-Up Costs?

Even the fixing up of properties in bad condition is negotiable. The REO officer may be aware that the property requires $10,000 in repair work. That may be knocked right off the top of the price. Or the lender may advance you the money to make repairs (meaning that once you bought the property, you would be getting additional money paid to you to fix it up). The money advanced could be added to your loan or could be an outright direct payment to you from the lender once the work is done. As I said, it's all negotiable.

How Do I Get the Best Deal?

To get the best deal, you first have to know what you want (price, terms, repairs, etc.) and then you have to find out what is the most the lender will give. As I've noted elsewhere, there are a lot of good books on the market dealing with negotiations. (You can try mine, *Tips and Traps When Negotiating Real Estate*, McGraw-Hill.) You can try the techniques these books offer.

Or you can simply ask. I've found that sometimes it works to tell the lender what would be the best deal for you. Offer so much down, so much a month, so much as an interest rate, specify the terms, and see what happens. If your offer is realistic, the lender may go along with it or only modify it slightly. In any event it is a point at which serious negotiations can begin.

Another way to approach negotiations is to ask the REO officer the following questions: How much will it take to get you out of this property? What's the lowest down payment (best interest rate, longest terms, highest repair allowance, etc.) you'll offer me if I take this property off your hands right now, today?

Once you've gotten to know the REO officer (after you've purchased your first property), things should move along more smoothly. He or she may offer you a selection of other properties. You might ask to see the "worst dogs" the officer has and make lowball offers on them. The possibilities are endless.

What Kinds of Problems Do REOs Have?

The problems with REOs are usually far less than for other repossessed property, but they do exist and can be severe on occasion. Frequently, the lender will pay for a policy of title insurance and will guarantee that your loan is indeed a first (no hidden liens) and that the title is clear.

TRAP

It's up to you to investigate the property thoroughly, usually before you make your offer. Know what you're buying. After the purchase you're probably stuck with it.

You are nevertheless buying a property that you must now take responsibility for. Frequently, these sales are "as is." This means that if the property is sliding down a hill and is about to be condemned, it could be your problem. If there's a tenant who won't pay and won't get out, that could be your problem too (although you could negotiate with the REO officer as a condition of your purchase that the property be vacant when you take ownership). If the property has termites, the lender may not correct the problem.

You may intend renting the property out (instead of buying and quickly reselling). You should do your homework to see that the potential rental income will cover the mortgage payments, taxes, insurance, and other costs.

In other words, the problems with REOs are usually the same as with buying any other investment property. Buying it from a bank usually, but not always, means that you're getting a fairly clean deal. Just because a lender is an institution doesn't mean, however, that it's looking out for your interests. You have to keep your eyes open and your mind alert in all real estate transactions.

Are REOs the Best Deals Around?

What's best for one person may not be right for another. As I've noted, REOs tend to be the cleanest deals around. Since they've already gone through the foreclosure process, many of the problems associated with title have been cleared up. Usually, but not always, the lender will give you clean title and a policy of title insurance. In addition, many times the properties themselves have either been cleaned up, or the lender will give you a clean-up allowance.

As a result REOs are frequently good bargains for the hunter who doesn't want to work too hard. The downside is that REOs often don't afford as big a bargain in terms of price (and profit) as some of the other opportunities in foreclosure we'll look at.

TRAP

Be sure to thoroughly check out the property (use a professional inspector) so you know what you are getting. Pay special attention to hazardous problems such as lead, asbestos, and black mold, as you may be responsible for a later expensive cleanup.

5
HUD Repos

Many investors begin their search for REOs in HUD repos. The Department of Housing and Urban Development (HUD) takes back homes that were insured by the Federal Housing Administration (FHA) and lost to foreclosure. Although technically these are REOs, they are commonly called HUD repos.

The FHA insures low down payment (3 percent) mortgages to those who qualify (the mortgages are offered by conventional lenders, such as banks). However, because the down payment is low, the buyer has almost no equity in the property. Thus, if times turn bad before the property has appreciated much in value, the borrower has great difficulty in reselling. Frequently, there isn't enough margin to cover the sales commission for an agent. Thus, a good many of these buyers default on their payments, and the lenders eventually foreclose. As part of the foreclosure process, HUD "buys" the properties back from the lenders. At any given time, there may be tens of thousands of homes nationwide owned by HUD and obtained in this manner.

Because the maximum FHA loan is fairly low (the amount varies from area to area, but the highest mortgage as of this writing is $208,800), the properties are typically moderate to low in value. These are often homes in modest neighborhoods. Some are in slums, but most are in blue-collar areas.

HUD disposes of the property through a program administered by regional property management companies. In California and parts of the West, for example, as of this writing the program is handled by Golden Feather Realty Services. In the Midwest it's First Preston. In New England it's handled by CitiWest.

However, you do not need to contact these property managers directly. Rather, purchases are handled by any local real estate broker. You go through a broker, who submits your offer to HUD. (HUD pays a real estate commission to the successful broker of up to 5 percent.)

TRAP

 HUD, as the seller, is only interested in what it will "net" out of the selling price. Remember, it has to pay a commission, and then there are some closing costs. This is important to keep in mind when making your offer. Because there's a broker involved, HUD will net significantly less than you offer. For example, if you offer $120,000 on a home, the net to HUD may be less a 5 percent commission and less $1000 in costs, or only $113,000. On the other hand, another offer may come in from a broker asking only a 4 percent commission. That's $1200 less in commission but $1200 more net for HUD: $113,000 from your offer and $114,200 from the other person even though both offers are for the same purchase price. For this reason your offer may not be accepted, even though the property is sold for the same price to someone else. Pay attention to what HUD receives as well as to what you're paying.

HUD typically goes through two "offer periods." The start and end of the first are normally well defined, and your broker can find out about them for you.

The first offer period is basically for "priority bidders." These are people who want to live in the home. Anyone who is willing to be an owner-occupant is given priority. Only if there are no owner-occupant bidders are offers from investors such as you considered.

TIP

Only licensed real estate agents can present your offer.

Sealed bids are presented to HUD during the offer period but are not opened. Only after the offer period has expired are the sealed bids opened. And assuming there are qualified buyers, HUD will basically accept the highest net offer. (Remember, that's the offer that yields it the highest price.)

On the other hand, if there are no bids, which sometimes happens, then it's investor time. You may now submit an offer at any time, including weekends. Your offer will be opened as it is received, and if HUD determines that it can live with the net you're presenting, you'll get the house. Typically, the broker of the successful buyer will be notified in 1 to 2 days.

On the other hand, if there are no offers HUD likes, it can wait, try a new offer period, or even on occasion go back to earlier offers that it had received but not accepted.

TIP

In some areas, if you're a teacher or a police officer and intend to move into the home, you can get as much as 50 percent off the price. Check below.

Should I Get an Appraisal First?

You should certainly check out the property and get a comparative market analysis (CMA) so that you know what similar properties have sold for. That should be your guide as to how much to bid.

Some bidders will offer close to market price. Others will try to sneak in with a low bid. Sometimes, if there's little interest in the house, the low bidder can walk away with it.

Are the Properties in Good Shape?

Generally, no, although they run a broad range of conditions. Remember, these homes were taken back through foreclosure. There was little or no incentive on the part of the former owners to maintain them during the long foreclosure process. In some cases vandalism may have taken place. Thus, you'd be well served to screen these properties carefully.

TRAP

Beware of "HUD slums." Sometimes FHA loans are made to an entire tract of homes. Later, many, and sometimes most, of the homeowners for one reason or another fall into foreclosure. Soon whole blocks of the tract are vacant HUD repos. On occasion vandalism runs rampant. Some of the homes may turn into "crack" houses. In short, the entire area becomes so depressed that it's not likely to be suitable for investment purposes.

All of the HUD homes are sold "as is." This means that HUD does not warrant their condition. Thus, it's up to you to conduct a thorough inspection. If you're serious about a home, you may even want to hire a professional home inspector to check it out. However, you'll have to pay the $250 to $300 inspection fee, and later, if you aren't the successful bidder, that's money down the drain.

What Are HUD Incentives?

- The asking price will typically reflect the condition of the property. For example, if the home in perfect condition might have a market value of $150,000 and this home needs $50,000 of corrective work, HUD would probably ask less than $100,000. If you can get it for less and do the work cheaply, you will have bought yourself a real bargain. (Beware of underestimating repair costs. Unless you're expert at remodeling and refurbishing, get bids from professionals.)

- HUD may offer a moving allowance to a successful bidder as an incentive to purchase a home (primarily for owner-occupants).

- If the property is particularly run-down, HUD may offer an upgrade allowance. I've seen these that were quite large, sometimes well over $10,000.

- HUD may offer a cash bonus for closing the deal early. Typical closings take anywhere from 30 to 60 days. Close in 15 days and HUD may be willing to pop for a few extra dollars.

While all of the incentives sound good, it's important to keep in mind that HUD's primary goal is to get as much money out of the properties as quickly as possible. Typically, the "good" properties will go fast, and there's little need for HUD to offer incentives on them. The "dogs" that won't move are more likely to offer incentives.

But then again, if you can buy a dog for a fraction of the market price, fix it up inexpensively, and resell for a hefty profit, those are just the properties you want!

Who Pays the Closing Costs?

The closing costs (not including the real estate agent's commission) amount to about 3 to 4 percent or less. Typically, the buyer would pay these, except that you can write into your offer that HUD pays most of them. If HUD accepts, you don't have to worry about the closing costs.

Keep in mind, however, that having HUD pay your closing costs means that it gets a lower net out of the deal, and your offer is less competitive than someone else's who doesn't ask HUD to pay closing costs.

What about Financing?

HUD offers financing through the FHA (which insures mortgages but does not generally make them). However, most of this financing is for owner-occupants.

As an investor, you'll probably need to come up with your own financing. Be sure to contact a lender first.

Where Do I Find
HUD Homes?

Begin your search for a HUD home by logging on to the Web. (As with most foreclosed properties today, the basic work is done on the Internet.)

The main HUD site is www.hud.org. However, as of this writing, the address that takes you to the homes for sale site is www.hud.gov/offices/hsg/sfh/reo/homes.cfm. This will give you a list of states. Pick your state and you'll be taken to the site of the real estate management company that oversees the area. Not all homes are listed on the Internet, but many are. You'll also be given some helpful information about buying homes from HUD.

Where Do I Find
a Participating Agent?

Basically, any licensed agent can participate in the program. However, agents must first register, and there are forms for them to fill out.

Some agents sell HUD properties on a regular basis and, therefore, are much more familiar with the process and are more likely to find what you want the first time out. An agent new to this area is more likely to bog you down and miss a successful bid.

To facilitate sales of these foreclosed homes, in some areas HUD will use broad listing brokers (BLBs). These are brokers who will list the properties on their local MLS. You can buy through them or through any other broker. However, the BLB gets a fee for handling some of the sales work on each transaction. A list of BLBs is available from the property manager in your area (found by going to your local sale site).

The HUD foreclosure homes for sale can be a good place to begin your search for hidden real estate bargains. Keep in mind that the program attempts to sell the properties for market price, so you'll have to be careful and patient to get one that's far below.

You can also contact HUD directly:

U.S. Department of Housing and Urban Development
451 7th St. SW
Washington, DC 20410
Telephone: (202) 708-1112   TTY: (202) 708-1455

6
VA Repos

The Veterans Administration also offers bargain hunting opportunities. It guarantees the purchase of homes by eligible veterans. This basically means that if the veteran defaults on the mortgage, the VA will pay off the lender and take the property back. Although technically these are REOs, they are commonly called VA repos.

VA repos are not found in high-priced areas because the VA maximum mortgage amount is fairly low by today's standards ($240,000). However, in modest to low-priced areas where they are found, they can be excellent opportunities for investors who are willing to buy properties "as is" and in poor condition and then fix them up. You may be able to buy a VA foreclosure for a fraction of its market price.

TRAP

Keep in mind that the VA sells properties "as is." It makes no warranties about the property's condition. Be sure that you have the property thoroughly checked by a competent professional home inspector. Pay particular attention to lead, black mold, and asbestos hazards, as you may be the one to pay for costly repairs.

VA foreclosures may sometimes impress you by how clean and neat they are. At other times you may be equally impressed by the run-down condition of the property.

Remember, these homes were taken back as part of a foreclosure procedure. The former owners were often months, sometimes years, in arrears in their mortgage payments. Often, they were in terrible financial condition, unable to handle even minimal maintenance and repairs. The properties may reflect this.

TIP

In actual practice the VA guarantees the top 25 percent of the mortgage to the lender. Upon default the lender forecloses to take the property back. As part of the foreclosure process, the lender notifies the VA that it is claiming the insurance. When this happens, the VA typically pays off the lender and assumes title to the property after foreclosure. The VA then offers these properties for sale to the public. Generally speaking, the VA gives clear title.

At any given time, the VA may own more than 20,000 properties scattered across the United States. (As of this writing, there were 21,066 in the VA's inventory. You can find the inventory by going to www.home loans.va.gov/homes.htm.)

Keep in mind that these are foreclosed properties, and some may not be in the best of condition. In fact, some may be in terrible condition.

Further, the VA offers these properties for sale "as is." It's up to you to determine what it will cost to fix them and bring them up to investment standards.

TRAP

Although you do have to be a veteran to buy a home using a VA loan (which offers nothing-down financing), you do not have to be a veteran to purchase one of these foreclosures. They are open to the general public.

The VA hopes to sell most of its homes to owner-occupants. It may, therefore, offer its own minimum down (as little as 2 percent) foreclosed property loan to people who intend to live in the property.

On the other hand, as an investor, the minimum down payment for VA financing is typically 10 percent. However, you are encouraged (by the VA) to secure your financing elsewhere.

Types of Housing

Most of the properties are single-family dwellings, although there may be an occasional multiple-family dwelling (usually no more than four units) thrown into the mix.

The VA has an internal system of coding for housing. There are basically four codes that I've seen it use in California and elsewhere. They include the following.

Code A. These are the better homes and, understandably, have better financing available. Typically, these are the homes that most owner-occupants will opt for. Financing includes VA special foreclosed property financing as well as veteran's loans (the type given to vets where the VA guarantees the properties, which is what got it into trouble in the first place). The VA will always accept cash from the buyer and in this case external financing as well.

Code C. These are usually pretty rough properties. The VA typically has marked them down in price for quick sale, and they are homes that investors should consider. However, keep in mind that the VA will only accept cash for these properties. No internal or external financing is allowed. (You can arrange for your own financing, but it's strictly cash to the VA, usually at the time of sale.)

TIP

If you can buy one of the VA homes for cash, there should be nothing to stop you from turning around and refinancing for a sizable mortgage once it's in your name. Of course, you'll have to find a willing lender.

Code T. These homes may be even rougher. However, for whatever reason, the VA will allow its own internal financing on them but not external financing. This means you can get a foreclosed property VA loan. However, time is of the essence. The VA wants these properties sold within 30 days (22 days if you go with their internal financing).

Code X. These are properties that for one reason or another will not qualify for either VA or FHA financing. However, you can get external financing from conventional lenders, pay cash, or use the VA's internal foreclosed property financing. The closing period can often be extended for up to 60 days.

Where Do I Find VA Homes?

Your best bet is to check with local brokers. The VA sells all its properties through brokers and pays a 6 percent commission. If you're in an area where VA properties are available, most brokers will know about them and be eager to help you make a purchase.

The sale is conducted by one of the VA's property management affiliates (see the list by state at the end of this chapter).

How Do I Submit an Offer?

As previously noted, you cannot submit an offer directly. It must be done through a real estate agent of your choice. The agent can contact the local VA property management company and secure a key to let you in and show you the home.

TRAP

In areas that have VA properties, there is often a game played by agents to find out which properties are going to be offered for sale before they are actually listed. This gives investors more time to refine their offer. However, the VA will not officially release any information on a property, including price, until it is listed and will not officially allow anyone, including agents, to go into the property until it is listed.

When the VA is ready, it will advertise the property under a "competitive listing" system. The advertisement, which may appear in local papers or which may be sent to real estate brokers, will indicate the term of the "competitive bid period."

All bids during this period are technically kept sealed and are not opened until the period ends. (I say technically because the bids may indeed be opened, but no priority is given to bids sent in earlier than other bids. They are all considered as simultaneously received by the VA as long as they are received during the bidding period.)

Depending on your area, the VA may require the bids to be sent by mail, electronically over the Internet, or by some other means. Your broker will know about this.

The VA will establish a minimum price as well as terms and conditions for the sale. The VA suggests that to be acceptable, all bids must meet the terms and conditions. During this period, only bids that meet the VA's price are usually considered.

Sometimes no acceptable bids will be received. When that happens, the VA typically opens the bidding as an "extended listing."

Now bids are first come, first served. As soon as the VA receives a bid it considers acceptable, it accepts it and the extended listing period ends. It is often at this time that investors get their best buys, as the VA is usually quite anxious to get rid of the property. Often, the VA will consider a price well below its set price. However, the terms and conditions of the sale (as noted earlier) are usually quite inflexible.

If no acceptable bid is received, the VA typically takes the home off the market for a time and then relists it on a new competitive bid listing at a new and usually lower price.

TIP

Old-timers who are used to offers and counteroffers will be disappointed by VA foreclosure sales. The VA will either accept or reject your offer. If will not argue with you in the form of counters. This means you must make your offer as desirable as possible the first time. Incentives for the VA to consider your offer over others are a price close to what they are asking (remember, they will consider a price reduction) and all or close to all cash. Offers that try to change the terms and conditions of the sale (for example, asking the VA to waive its "as is" policy) are likely to be rejected.

To find out more about VA homes for sale, you can contact the VA at any of its offices, or you may use their Web site: www.va.gov.

For information on foreclosures, you should check with a local real estate broker. You may also want to check with their local management agency. These are listed by state:

VA Offices by State

Alabama
VA Regional Office
345 Perry Hill Rd.
Montgomery, AL 36109
www.vamontgomery.com
RBBS (334) 213-3424

Alaska
VA Regional Office
2925 Debarr Rd.
Anchorage, AK 99508
www.vaalaska.com

Arizona
VA Regional Office
3225 N Central Ave.
Phoenix, AZ 85012
www.vahomes.org/pn/
Faxback (602) 530-3574

Arkansas
VA Regional Office
PO Box 1280, Fort Roots
N Little Rock, AR 72115
www.vahomes.org/lr/

California (southern, except San
    Diego area)
VA Regional Office
11200 Wilshire Blvd.
Los Angeles, CA 90024
www.vahomes.org/la/
Faxback (800) 479-5658

California (northern and northern
    Nevada)
VA Regional Office
1301 Clay St., 1300 North
Oakland, CA 94612-5209
www.vba.va.gov/ro/oakland/index.
    html

California (San Diego area)
VA Regional Office
8810 Rio San Diego Dr.
San Diego, CA 92108
www.vasandiego.com

Colorado
VA Regional Loan Center
155 Van Gordon St.
Lakewood, CO 80228
www.vba.va.gov/ro/denver/
    index.htm
Faxback (888) 523-4286

Connecticut (see also New
    England)
VA Regional Office
275 Chestnut St.
Manchester, NH 03101

Delaware (see also Pennsylvania,
    eastern)
VARO & Insurance Center
5000 Wissahickon Ave.
Philadelphia, PA 19101

Dist. of Columbia (northern VA,
    & Mont. & PG Counties in MD)
VA Regional Office
1120 Vermont Ave. NW
Washington, DC 20421
www.vahomeswash.com
Faxback (202) 269-2076

Florida
VA Regional Office
PO Box 1437
St. Petersburg, FL 33731
www.vaflorida.com

Georgia
Department of Veterans Affairs
Regional Loan Center
1700 Clairmont Rd.
PO Box 100023
Decatur, GA 30031-7023
www.vba.va.gov/ro/atlanta/rlc/
    index.htm
Polled Fax (888) 768-2132 x3067

Hawaii
VA Med & RO Center
459 Patterson Rd.
Honolulu, HI 96819-1522
(808) 433-0483

Idaho
VA Regional Office
805 W Franklin St.
Boise, ID 83702-5560
www.vba-boi-lgy.com

Illinois
VA Regional Office
PO Box 8136
Chicago, IL 60680
www.vahomes.org/ch/
RBBS24 (312) 353-2382

Indiana
VA Regional Office
575 Pennsylvania St.
Indianapolis, IN 46204-1541
www.vba.va.gov/ro/central/indy/
　index.htm

Iowa
VA Regional Office
210 Walnut St.
Des Moines, IA 50309
www.vba.va.gov/ro/desmoines/
　index.html

Kansas
VA Med & RO Center
PO Box 20077
Wichita, KS 67208-1077
www.vahomes.org/ks

Kentucky
VA Regional Office
545 S 3rd St.
Louisville, KY 40202
www.vba.va.gov/ro/central/louvl/
　LOAN/Cover.htm

Louisiana
VA Regional Office
701 Loyola Ave.
New Orleans, LA 70113
mirage.towerauction.net/no

Maine (see also New England)
VA Regional Office
275 Chestnut St.
Manchester, NH 03101

Maryland (except PG and Mont.
　Counties; see DC)
VA Regional Office
31 Hopkins Plaza
Baltimore, MD 21201
www.vahomes.org/bt/
Faxback (410) 962-7874

Massachusetts (see also New
　England)
VA Regional Office
275 Chestnut St.
Manchester, NH 03101

Michigan
VA Regional Office
477 Michigan Ave.
Detroit, MI 48226
www.vba.va.gov/ro/central/detr/
　default.htm
RBBS (313) 226-4227

Minnesota
VARO & Insurance Center
Fort Snelling
St. Paul, MN 55111
www.vba.va.gov/ro/central/stpau/
　pages/prpmanag.html
(800) 827-0633

Mississippi
VA Regional Office
1600 E Woodrow Wilson Ave.
Jackson, MS 39216
www.vba.va.gov/ro/south/jacks/
　LGYListings/LGY.htm

Missouri
VA Regional Office
400 S 18th St.
St. Louis, MO 63103-2271
www.vahomes.org/sl/

Montana (see also Colorado)
VA Regional Loan Center
155 Van Gordon St.
Lakewood, CO 80228

Nebraska
VA Regional Office
5631 S 48th St.
Lincoln, NE 68516
(402) 421-7480
RBBS (402) 420-4068

Nevada (northern; see also California, northern)
VA Regional Office
1301 Clay St., 1300 North
Oakland, CA 94612-5209

Nevada (southern; see also Arizona)
VA Regional Office
3225 N Central Ave.
Phoenix, AZ 85012

New England
VA Regional Office
275 Chestnut St.
Manchester, NH 03101
www.vba.va.gov/ro/manchester/
  lgymain/loans.html
(800) 827-6311

New Hampshire
VA Regional Office
275 Chestnut St.
Manchester, NH 03101
www.vba.va.gov/ro/manchester/
  lgymain/loans.html
(800) 827-6311

New Jersey
VA Regional Office
20 Washington Place
Newark, NJ 07102
www.vba.va.gov/ro/east/newrk/
  lgy/index.htm
Faxback (973) 297-4808

New Mexico
VA Regional Office
PO Box 0968
Albuquerque, NM 87102
(505) 248-6680

New York (western)
VA Regional Office
111 W Huron St.
Buffalo, NY 14202
(716) 551-5295

New York (eastern)
VA Regional Office
245 West Houston St.
New York, NY 10014
www.vba.va.gov/ro/east/ny/
  LGYHome.htm

North Carolina
VA Regional Office
251 N Main St.
Winston Salem, NC 27155
www.vancprop.com

North Dakota
VARO & Insurance Center
Fort Snelling
St. Paul, MN 55111

Ohio
VA Regional Office
1240 E 9th St.
Cleveland, OH 44199
www.vba.va.gov/ro/central/cleve/
  index1.htm

Oklahoma
VA Regional Office
125 Main St.
Muskogee, OK 74401
http://www.gibill.va.gov/
  muskogee/lg.htm
RBBS (918) 687-2364

Oregon
VA Regional Office
1220 SW 3rd Ave.
Portland, OR 97204
www.pmlgyport.com
(503) 326-2457

Pennsylvania (western)
VA Regional Office
1000 Liberty Ave.
Pittsburgh, PA 15222
www.vba.va.gov/ro/east/pitts/loan/
  default.htm

Pennsylvania (eastern)
VARO & Insurance Center
5000 Wissahickon Ave.
Philadelphia, PA 19101
www.vba.va.gov/philly.htm

Puerto Rico
VA Regional Office
GPO Box 4867
San Juan, PR 00936
(787) 766-5177

Rhode Island (see also New England)
VA Regional Office
275 Chestnut St.
Manchester, NH 03101

South Carolina
VA Regional Office
1801 Assembly St.
Columbia, SC 29201
www.vba.va.gov/columbia-ro.htm
Faxback (803) 255-4136

South Dakota
VARO & Insurance Center
Fort Snelling
St. Paul, MN 55111

Tennessee
VA Regional Office
110 9th Ave. S
Nashville, TN 37203
www.vanashpm.vol.com

Texas (southern)
VA Regional Office
6900 Alemda Rd.
Houston, TX 77030
www.vahouston.com

Texas (northern)
VA Regional Office
1 Veterans Plaza, 701 Clay St.
Waco, TX 76799
www.vawaco.com

Utah
VA Regional Office
PO Box 11500
Salt Lake City, UT 84147
www.vbaslc.com

Vermont (see also New England)
VA Regional Office
275 Chestnut St.
Manchester, NH 03101

Virginia (except northern VA; see also DC)
VA Regional Office
210 Franklin Rd. SW
Roanoke, VA 24011
www.vba-roanoke.com/rlc
RBBS (540) 857-2735

Washington State
VA Regional Office
915 2nd Ave.
Seattle, WA 98174
www.seattleva.com

West Virginia (see also Virginia)
VA Regional Office
210 Franklin Rd., SW
Roanoke, VA 24011

Wisconsin
VA Regional Office
5000 National Ave.
Milwaukee, WI 53295
(414) 382-5060

Wyoming (see also Colorado)
VA Regional Loan Center
155 Van Gordon St.
Lakewood, CO 80228

7
Fannie Mae and Freddie Mac REOs

Although real estate mortgages are funded through banks, mortgage bankers, and other financial lending institutions, in most cases the money actually comes from two giant secondary lenders: Fannie Mae and Freddie Mac.

These are quasi-public organizations that create a secondary market for residential real estate loans. This means that when a bank creates a mortgage, it can then "sell" that mortgage to Fannie Mae or Freddie Mac and recoup most of its investment, which it can then loan out again. It continues to service the loan (collect the payments) for a fee, although it can also sell this servicing to some other similar organization if it chooses. (This is why, if you've ever had one of these mortgages, you find that the lender to whom you make payments is constantly changing.)

However, to sell a mortgage to Fannie Mae or Freddie Mac, the mortgage must conform to the underwriting criteria of these organizations. (Hence, these are called *conforming loans*.) Although it is not necessary to explain these criteria in this book (you can check my recent book, *How to Buy a Home When You Can't Afford a Home*, for details), the one criterion that is important here is the maximum loan amount. This amount frequently changes, but as of this writing, the maximum is $307,000. In previous years it was much lower. This means that all the mortgages underwritten by Fannie Mae and Freddie Mac will be low to moderate in size, as will the market value of the properties on which these loans were made.

Although the underwriting practices of these two giants are probably the best in the world, including the use of a highly sophisticated financial database and computer analysis programs, sometimes borrowers find they can't make the payments, can't sell, and so lose their property to foreclosure. When this happens, Fannie Mae and Freddie Mac pick up the properties and then turn them around and try to resell them. Their goal is to minimize their loss, meaning they try to get the highest prices for them.

TIP

Unlike HUD properties, which tend to be grouped together, Fannie Mae and Freddie Mac REOs are scattered all over the country. Very likely there is one in a neighborhood near you.

Both Fannie Mae and Freddie Mac sell their homes through local real estate agents. To make an offer, you must contact the agent.

Generally speaking, they prefer to sell to owner-occupants. However, particularly if the property is very rough, they do sell to investors.

As an investor, you are probably better off securing your own financing. You can try for a conforming loan. However, you may find that many of these properties will no longer qualify in their current condition, so other financing may be necessary.

Where Can I Find Freddie Mac Properties?

Freddie Mac sells its properties through its HomeSteps program. This is designed to help first-time and low-income homeowners get into houses. You can find information about it on the Internet at www.homesteps.com.

The organization will provide some helpful tips on home purchases. But more important, it will help you find homes that it has for sale and agents who are approved to work for it.

At the site, by putting in the size, city or county, and price of the home you're looking for, you'll be given access to the Freddie Mac database listing available homes that fall under those parameters. You'll be told the location of the property, the asking price, be given a map of the area, and told the real estate company that's handling the sale. After that you're on your own to contact the agent and go out and see the property.

TIP

In talking with a Freddie Mac representative in Virginia, I was told that in 2001 the organization only had between 6000 and 7000 REOs for sale. This was down considerably from the 10,000 plus it had for sale during the real estate recession years of the 1990s. The number of homes available tends to vary depending on the economy and the overall real estate market.

If you want to contact Freddie Mac directly, here's a list of some of its larger offices:

Headquarters I
8200 Jones Branch Dr.
McLean, VA 22102-3110
(703) 903-2000

Headquarters II
8250 Jones Branch Dr.
McLean, VA 22102-3110
(703) 918-5000

Headquarters III
8100 Jones Branch Dr.
McLean, VA 22102-3110
(703) 714-2500

New York City Office
575 Lexington Ave.
Suite 1800
New York, NY 10022-6102
(212) 418-8900

Northeastern Region
1410 Springhill Rd.
Suite 600
PO Box 50122
McLean, VA 22102-8922
(703) 902-7700

Northern Central Region
333 W Wacker Dr.
Suite 2500
Chicago, IL 60606-1287
(312) 407-7400

Southeastern Region
N Tower Suite 200
2300 Windy Ridge Pkwy. SE
Atlanta, GA 30339-5671
(770) 857-8800

Southwestern Region
5000 Plano Pkwy.
Carrollton, TX 75010
(972) 395-4000

Western Region
21700 Oxnard St.
Suite 1900
Woodland Hills, CA 91367-3621
(818) 710-3000

Where Can I Find Fannie Mae Properties?

Fannie Mae offers its property through its HomePath organization. This is its home management division operating throughout the United States.

To find a Fannie Mae home in your area, go to the Internet and type www.fanniemae.com/homes. This takes you to their HomePath site.

Here you are asked for the parameters of the home you are searching for. You can list your price range, city, and home type. Then you'll be shown an index of Fannie Mae REOs available in your area. You'll also be told the name of the real estate agency that's handling them and be given the option of seeing a map showing the property's location.

All Fannie Mae properties are listed with agents and are on the multiple-listing service (MLS). As with Freddie Mac, the primary goal is to sell the properties to owner-occupants. Barring that, however, it can sell to investors.

It's now up to you to contact the agent to view the property and go from there with making an offer.

You can also contact Fannie Mae at:

Corporate Headquarters
Fannie Mae
3900 Wisconsin Ave., NW
Washington, DC 20016-2892
(202) 752-7000

Southeastern Regional Office
Fannie Mae
950 E Pacs Ferry Rd.
Atlanta, GA 30326-1161
(404) 398-6000
Areas served: Alabama, District of
Columbia, Florida, Georgia, Ken-
tucky, Maryland, Mississippi,
North Carolina, South Carolina,
Tennessee, Virginia, West Virginia

Midwestern Regional Office
Fannie Mae
1 S Wacker Dr.
Suite 1300
Chicago, IL 60606-4667
(312) 368-6200
Areas served: Illinois, Indiana, Iowa,
Michigan, Minnesota, Nebraska,
North Dakota, Ohio, South
Dakota, Wisconsin

Southwestern Regional Office
Fannie Mae
2 Galleria Tower
13455 Noel Rd.
Suite 600
Dallas, TX 75240-5003
(973) 773-HOME
Areas served: Arizona, Arkansas,
Colorado, Kansas, Louisiana, Mis-
souri, New Mexico, Oklahoma,
Texas, Utah

Western Regional Office
Fannie Mae
135 N Los Robles Ave.
Suite 300
Pasadena, CA 91101-1707
(626) 396-5100
Areas served: Alaska, California,
Guam, Hawaii, Idaho, Montana,
Nevada, Oregon, Washington,
Wyoming

Northeastern Regional Office
Fannie Mae
1900 Market St.
Suite 800
Philadelphia, PA 19103
(215) 575-1400
Areas served: Connecticut,
Delaware, Maine, Massachusetts,
New Hampshire, New Jersey, New
York, Pennsylvania, Puerto Rico,
Rhode Island, Vermont, Virgin
Islands

8

GSA and IRS Auctions

The General Services Administration (GSA) sells surplus real estate owned by the government. This property is acquired from a wide variety of sources. Some comes from the Internal Revenue Service (IRS), which acquires property from people who don't pay their federal income taxes (discussed later). Other properties come from other agencies of the federal government. The Property Disposal Office of the GSA has the responsibility of selling property to the highest bidder. Sometimes you can get extraordinary bargains here.

The GSA usually sells its properties using two methods: sealed bid and public auction.

In the sealed bid method, bidders are directed to mail their bids with a designated minimum deposit to a specified regional office. You must get the bid in prior to the opening time.

When the time for opening bids arrives, all sealed bids are opened. This procedure is open to the public. The property goes to the highest bidder. However, the GSA reserves the right not to sell the property if all of the bids are significantly below the market price of the real estate.

TRAP

If you send in a sealed bid, you may be able to modify it by sending in a second bid prior to the opening of all bids. However, once the opening has started, you can't modify your bids.

There are three types of public auction. At the oral auction, a date, time, and place are specified by the GSA. You have to show up with the required bid deposit. An auctioneer handles the bidding, and you bid against others for the property. The highest bid wins.

A second kind of auction is also held in which you may increase your bids by sending e-mail, fax, mail, online, or in-person bids. This auction is held over a period of days until there are no additional bidders willing to raise their bid. Then the high bidder is awarded the property. Again, if all bids are too low, the GSA reserves the right to cancel the auction because the price does not represent the fair market value of the property. If it cancels, it may hold another auction at a later date.

TIP

GSA properties are generally sold on a cash only basis. This does not mean you cannot get financing. It does mean you're on your own to arrange financing before the bidding.

Finally, the GSA also holds online auctions. Here all activities, including submission of bids and increasing the bid amount, are handled online. As before, the auction continues for a period of days until a high bidder emerges. For more information on online auctions, go to www.auctionrp. com/.

What Types of Property Does the GSA Offer for Sale?

Because the GSA draws from throughout the federal government, the types of properties are varied. They include:

Land

Industrial

Commercial

Residential

Retail

In addition the properties are scattered across the country. To find out what GSA properties are available in your area, point your Web browser to propertydisposal.gsa.gov/Property/.

Furthermore, the GSA often has "hot" properties that it is anxious to dispose of. You can read a description of these at the Web site just given.

When you designate a city or area of the country you wish to find out about, you'll be told about the property, the minimum suggested bid, and the date, time, place, and method of auction.

Investors Wanted

As of this writing, the GSA is looking for investors to help with its auctions of IRS property. It wants investors to underwrite these by agreeing to support minimum bids.

The way it works is that you guarantee to purchase the property at a minimum bid price. You get a list of available properties that includes a description of the property, the minimum bid price, and the expiration date of the bidding.

TIP

The GSA will provide a title report, an assessed value, and the cost of utilities and other items. But you have to get this directly from the local office representing the property. Unfortunately, you often will not be allowed to inspect the properties in advance.

All you need to do is give the GSA a check for $5, and they will send you a registration packet. Then you can become the minimum bidder. At the auction you can let the minimum price stand and be outbid. Or if there is other bidding, you can bid again. However, if there is no other bidding, you've bought the property for the minimum bid. However, for agreeing to be the minimum bidder, the GSA will give you an "award."

Therefore, you must be very careful! Unless you want to own the property at the GSA's price, don't bid on it. Check it out at <u>propertydisposal.gsa.gov/ Property/IRS/</u>.

TRAP

These properties are generally acquired from the IRS. You'll get a deed, but there is no guarantee that the property does not have other liens or encumbrances. In other words, the sale could be subject to a previous mortgage. Also, as noted in Chapter 15 on inspections, be sure to check out the title thoroughly.

Where Can I Find Out about IRS Properties?

The IRS lists property it has seized and is offering for sale on its Web site www.treas.gov/auctions/irs/real1.html.

Generally, there are fewer than 100 properties at any given time, and they are scattered across the country. The terms for each piece vary, but the IRS usually wants a 20 percent deposit with your bid and all cash at the time of the sale. Cash means cash, certified check, cashier's check, or some similar form of payment. The bidding procedures also vary somewhat, but they are outlined for each property. When you click on the notice, you are told whom to contact, the bidding procedure, and photos of the real estate are given.

Because this property has been seized, it is not strictly in the same category as other REOs. Here are the basic terms of property offered by the IRS.

Title

The property is offered "as is" and "where is," which essentially mean that you take it with no right to rescind the purchase agreement later if you find that the property was not what you anticipated. The IRS offers no assurance as to the fitness of the property for any use.

The IRS will offer title to the property. However, it may not be clear title. When it takes a property, the IRS effectively wipes out any junior liens—that is, any liens placed on the property after the seizure. However, it does not necessarily affect any legitimate superior liens and mortgages— that is, those placed on the property prior to the seizure. For example, the property could be subject to a first, second, or other mortgage. The IRS will provide what information it has on these prior liens, but you're warned to check the title yourself (see also Chapter 3).

Redemption Period

Unlike most REOs, IRS property has a redemption period. This means that after the sale, the former owners or their heirs, executors or administrators, or any other person who had a lien or interest on the property has 180 days to redeem it. This right of redemption means they can demand and receive title back to the property you bought.

At first glance this may seem like a good reason not to buy IRS property, but it actually can be a plus. The reason is that to redeem it, the person who wants it back must pay you, the purchaser, your full price *plus 20 percent interest* per annum. In other words, if your property gets redeemed, you receive a payment of 20 percent a year for your troubles.

TIP

Many people buy IRS property in the hope that it will be redeemed. They are more interested in the 20 percent redemption payment than in reselling.

TRAP

You will not want to spend any money fixing up the property during the redemption period, as that money could be wasted if it is eventually redeemed. You may also find it difficult to resell the property during the redemption period.

There are investors who make their living bidding and buying IRS seized property. You too may want to join their ranks. However, keep in mind that because of the nature of the title given and the redemption period, this is not like buying most other types of REOs. You should study the properties to make sure that you're not paying too much and that it's actually a bargain. And you should study the IRS procedure so that you truly understand what you are getting yourself into.

9

SBA, Treasury, Army Corps of Engineers, and More

There are several other government entities where you may find bargains.

Small Business Administration

The U.S. Small Business Administration (SBA) offers loan programs to small businesses across the country. These businesses vary enormously from farms to commercial to residential properties.

As is the case elsewhere, when the borrowers can't make their payments, the SBA takes the property back. It then sells it to the public. The Web site to check is appl.sba.gov/pfsales/dsp_search.html.

This will take you to the SBA's search engine, where you can see what properties are currently available. At any given time, there may be relatively few pieces. However, they can be unusual. For example, the last time I was looking in California, the SBA was offering two commercial buildings: a warehouse and a microbrewery.

Each offering includes the contact person and a phone number. Just call and ask for details. You will be told the procedure used at the time and how to bid.

If you want to contact the SBA directly, you will need to check at this Web site for local phone numbers. The SBA maintains offices in every state, and the numbers for property sales are listed there. Check www.sba.gov/regions/states.html.

Treasury Department

The Treasury acquires properties from a variety of sources and then auctions them to the public. These are open auctions, and you do not need a real estate broker to participate. In addition the Treasury usually issues a clear, insured title to the buyer.

TIP

Unless otherwise specified, the Treasury will usually pay for all back taxes, liens, and title insurance on the properties.

To participate in these sales, you need to check the properties found on the Web at www.treas.gov/auctions/customs/realprop.html.

Unfortunately, there tend to be few properties offered for sale, but they can be anything from bare land to warehouses to airport hangars.

Once you find a property you're interested in, you need to call the Treasury's public auction line at (703) 361-3131 x279. You will then be sent a brochure on the property. Before bidding, however, you should carefully read the rules for the auction found (as of this writing) at www.treas.gov/auctions/customs/rpterms2.html.

Generally speaking, the properties are offered "as is" and "with all faults." However, you can make arrangements prior to bidding to inspect the properties.

Written bids must be submitted to the appropriate office along with a deposit. The Treasury does not handle any financing, but it will usually allow you up to 30 days to get financing to close the deal. Usually, you are notified by e-mail if you're the successful bidder.

TRAP

These are generally "reserve" auctions. This means the government has established a minimum bid. If that minimum bid is not achieved, it will not sell the property. In a few cases, however, it may offer "absolute" auctions in which the lowest price takes the property regardless. Check with the particular auction.

Army Corps of Engineers

The Corps acquires property in the course of creating many of its projects around the country. At any given time, however, there may be few or many properties for sale. Your best bet is to check their Web site at www.sas.usace.army.mil/hapinv/$rangech.htm.

Other Bargain Offerings

The U.S. Marshals Service and some local counties and cities use a service called Bid4Assets to handle their tax and seized asset disposal. It is located on the Web at www.bid4assets.com/.

Bid4Assets is a private company that handles online auctions for a wide variety of properties. You can bid on bare land, a house, a warehouse, or almost anything else. The auctions are held online with a certain cutoff time, and the property goes to the highest bidder. Remember, however, that you're dealing with both a private online auction company and in many cases a private or government seller. Use the same investigation and discretion that you would with any independent real estate purchase.

TRAP

Be careful! It can be a lot of fun bidding on a property in the middle of an Arizona desert when the price is only a few hundred dollars. But that property may have no water, no utilities, no roads leading to it, and may have a high tax burden. Be sure you thoroughly investigate what you're bidding on before you make your bid or else you might rue the day you win!

10
Private Individual's REOs

Thus far, we've considered REOs that were owned by lenders such as banks or by government agencies such as the VA or FHA (properties more often called repos). Now let's consider one category that most bargain hunters completely overlook. I call it "private REOs."

A Private Headache

There are many individuals who become involved in real estate repossessions unexpectedly and in an unwanted fashion. For example, Fred took back a second mortgage for $10,000 on his house 3 years ago. He thought he was through with the property.

But when it came time for the buyer to pay off the balloon on the second, the person defaulted. Fred was forced to start foreclosure proceedings and take back the property. Now Fred has a real headache.

During those 3 years, the former owner had rented the property out. The tenants didn't take care of it, and now it's a mess. The carpeting is ruined. There are holes in the walls. The toilet bowl is cracked. The house needs paint inside and out.

What's worse, since Fred originally sold the property, he has moved and now lives 300 miles away. He can't be there to do the work himself or even to supervise it. The final straw is that he's now making payments on an empty house.

Fred doesn't want to be a real estate landlord with the headaches involved. He doesn't want to own property far from where he lives. So he's thinking about how to get rid of it.

Fred's Eventual Solution

His logical answer, as soon as he thinks it through, will probably be to list the property with a local agent. He will hope to sell the problem away.

However, there are going to be problems selling a distressed house. The agent will undoubtedly first inform him what the price would be *if* the property were in tiptop shape. But the price will have to be reduced. The price a house can get is in large part determined by how well it "shows" to prospective buyers. A distressed house shows badly; hence, the price has to be lowered to compensate for this fact.

The Figures Speak for Themselves

Fred originally sold the property for $100,000 and got $15,000 down from the buyer. Since then, properties have gone up by perhaps $5000 in his area. Thus, he theoretically has a $20,000 equity after repossession.

However, there's the deduction for the way the house shows and the cost of the agent's commission (about $6300 if it's 6 percent). Fred realizes that he'll probably make a few bucks if he sells it right away. On the other hand, every month that drags by means he's making payments on the first mortgage ($800 per month) plus payments for taxes, insurance, and utilities.

What Fred Would Really Like to Do

Fred would really like to junk the property. If someone would take it off his hands, he'd probably be willing to let it go for what he has in it (the $10,000 second mortgage plus his costs of repossession). Fred is a bargain opportunity for the asking.

Finding the Bargain

Fred's house offers the bargain hunter an opportunity to do Fred a favor while at the same time picking up a substantial equity with little or no money down. The essence of making it work, however, is locating Fred before he lists the house.

Finding people like Fred is the same as finding REOs. It's a matter of checking to see what properties are sold in foreclosure sales and then contacting the lenders who foreclosed. Most will be S&Ls, but among the bunch will be a few Freds.

Taking Advantage of the Bargain

There are several ways that a bargain hunter could structure a purchase of Fred's property. Here are two.

Plan 1

Offer to pay Fred in cash for all his costs of foreclosure (probably a few thousand dollars) if he will give you title to the property and a new second trust deed for the original $10,000.

This isn't a bad offer, although it doesn't entirely get rid of the property for Fred. It pays back his out-of-pocket expenses. And he hasn't lost a dime because the same second is back on the house. The only danger to him is that you won't pay when the second comes due, and he'll have to foreclose and go through the whole hassle again. But that possibility is sometime in the future, and you're promising to remove his headache right now.

Plan 2

Offer to pay Fred in cash for all his costs of foreclosure and also give him $7000 in cash for his $10,000 second.

Not a bad offer. Fred gets his foreclosure costs back plus $7000 in cash. And he gets to walk away from the house. Considering the problems involved, it's a quick solution that Fred might take.

How much does plan 2 cost you? Nothing!

You write the deal so that you can paint and fix up the house in escrow before the sale. Once you've fixed the house up, you refinance it as part of the transaction. Your new loan is 90 percent of the market value:

Market value (after cosmetic repairs)	$105,000
Loan percentage (90%)	× 0.9
Loan amount you get	$94,500

You get about $94,000 from the refinancing and spend it in this fashion:

Pay off original first (it's gone down $2000 during the 3 years since Fred originally sold)	$68,000
Pay off Fred ($7000 for second plus $3000 for foreclosure costs)	10,000
Cosmetic repairs to property	3,500
Costs of purchase (loan points, etc.)	1,500
Total costs	$83,000
In your pocket after deal closes!	$11,000

Refinancing allows you to acquire the property with an equity of $11,000 and at the same time puts $11,000 in cash back in your pocket. Now that's a bargain!

Can I Do It?

All it takes is finding someone with a problem like Fred's. I can assure you that such people are everywhere around us. For Fred the property was the worst kind of headache. For you it can be one of the best bargains.

TRAP

Be sure you get title insurance on the property and handle the sale through an escrow. Don't trust Fred. He might not be honest and could add a lien to the property without telling you.

Also, as always, check for problems of occupancy.

Finally, be sure you know what repair problems are required and that you can handle them (see Chapter 15).

The Bottom Line

Private REOs are great when you can find them. But I would be less than honest to say that they are easy to find or that you will run into them every day. These properties take hard work and lots of it. But there are bargains to be had.

11

How to Buy at Auction

It's what people always think of when foreclosures are mentioned. The auctioneer, the gavel, the bidders, and the frenzy of pushing up the price. It's usually not as dramatic as that, but there's no question that auctions are the glamour area of foreclosures. It's here that properties go to the highest bidder. It's also here that some of the best buys can be obtained.

In a recent week in the Los Angeles area, I saw a condo worth $225,000 go for $187,000 and a house worth $335,000 go for $220,000. There's no question that the bargains are here.

However, right at the outset, it must be understood that this is also one of the riskiest areas of foreclosure to deal with. Many times it involves bidding blindly and hoping that you're doing the right thing. If you don't like taking risks, you don't belong at foreclosure sales.

It also usually involves either having a lot of cash, establishing a strong line of credit from a bank (which is equivalent to having cash), or setting up financing in advance. If you don't have money or strong financing, you don't belong at foreclosure auctions either.

Having thus glimpsed at the problems, let's see how to find the benefits.

TRAP

Bidding at auction is inherently risky. Further, that risk is amplified if you are new to the process. Therefore, in addition to the material presented in this chapter, you should also check for pitfalls and problems with a good attorney and/or real estate agent who participates in auctions on a regular basis. If at all possible, preview several auctions before actually bidding. Doing your homework here can save you a bundle later.

How a Foreclosure Auction Works

You'll recall from Chapter 3 that there are three stages to the foreclosure process. In the first stage, the borrower-owner is in default. If we buy then, we buy directly from this person.

In the last stage, the lender has taken the property back after a foreclosure auction—we're buying an REO property (see Chapter 4).

At the auction—stage 2—we're in the middle. This is where the borrower-owner loses the property and the lender acquires it. Here we can step in and snatch that property up at the sale.

TIP

The foreclosure process differs from state to state. However, in all cases, at some point there is a public auction, whether it be held by a trustee, a judge, a magistrate, or a referee. The property is auctioned off to the highest bidder.

In Trust Deed States

Using California as an example (a good many states are modeled after California), the foreclosure process uses a trust deed (sometimes called a *power of sale*) and normally takes place outside a court (although court foreclosure is allowed as a lender's option).

In California the first step is for the lender, called the beneficiary, to file a "notice of default" (see Chapter 3). Once this notice of default is filed, the owner-borrower has 90 days in which to make up any delinquent mortgage payments, interest, and penalties. If these are made up, the mortgage is reinstated, and the parties involved go their separate ways.

Once the 90-day reinstatement period has passed, however, the situation changes. Now there is a period of 21 days during which the trustee advertises the property in a newspaper, announcing the coming sale. (This is usually in a legal paper, which often turns out to be a tiny one that few people read.)

During the 21-day period, the owner-borrower may redeem the property by paying up all the delinquent payments and penalties and paying back the entire amount of the mortgage. Notice that paying only the back payments, interest, and penalties is not enough at this stage.

After this the trustee, to whom the borrower or beneficiary originally gave a power of sale, sells the house to the highest bidder "on the courthouse steps," which can be any public place (such as a courtroom). The place and time of the sale, however, must be publicly announced in the advertisement.

TIP

Auctioning by use of the power of sale given the trustee is at the lender's option. The lender may decide not to go through a trustee's foreclosure but instead to go through judicial foreclosure. Why would a lender opt for the longer and more costly judicial process? The reason would be that the lender felt the property could not bring enough money at sale to pay off the mortgage balance. By going through a judicial foreclosure, the lender can now go after the borrower personally. After a judicial foreclosure, if the property does not bring enough money at auction to cover the mortgage and costs, the lender may sue the borrower for any deficiency. If the lender prevails, a deficiency judgment can be issued by the court, which will hold the borrower personally responsible for the remaining debt. (Some states have "purchase money laws" in which a deficiency judgment may not be obtained when the mortgage was used as part of the original purchase price.)

In Judicial Foreclosure States

At one time all states used judicial foreclosure. Now, however, only a handful do. (The trustee sale process grew out of a common need for a swifter, less costly procedure.)

Although the process differs from state to state, generally speaking there are five steps:

1. The lender gives the borrower notice that he or she is in arrears and must make up the back payments.

2. The lender initiates foreclosure by filing a complaint in the county or township where the property is located and the deed is recorded. The borrower must be served with a notice of the complaint. Typically, the sheriff does this. The lender's attorney also will typically record a *lis pen-*

dens notice, which alerts everyone, including bargain hunters, that a property is in foreclosure.

3. Eventually, a court date will be set, and the lender and the borrower can come and present their cases. The lender's case almost always is that the borrower failed to perform by making the mortgage payments. The borrower usually doesn't show up, and in that case the judge issues a judgment which sets an amount that usually includes the unpaid balance of the mortgage along with interest due and costs. Now the borrower can no longer reinstate the mortgage by making up back payments. He or she can only save the property by paying off this total amount. The judgment also usually sets a date for a court sale of the property.

   Sometimes, however, the borrower-owner does show up and pleads extenuating circumstances such as loss of a job, illness, divorce, or whatever. The lender will claim that the property is a wasting asset and no time must be lost, but sometimes judges will give the person time (days, weeks, sometimes months) to get back on their feet and reinstate the mortgage.

4. Advertisement in a legal paper lets the public know that the property is going to be sold. The time allowed before the sale differs markedly from state to state.

5. Finally, the property is auctioned on the courthouse steps to the highest bidder. Some states have a redemption period, noted earlier, during which the former borrower-owner can sometimes live in the property and can redeem it by paying back the bidder's price plus interest.

TRAP

Depending on the state, the successful bidder may not get completely clear title. For example, many states that have judicial foreclosure also offer the original borrower-owner a right of redemption that can extend for many months. That person can, during this period, come back and redeem the property by paying the auction price plus interest at a hefty rate on that money. In trust deed states, on the other hand, there is normally no right of redemption after the auction sale. Be sure you check with an attorney for exactly how the procedure is handled in your state.

How Do I Find Property Up for Auction?

To find out which properties are going up for auction, you should read the local legal newspaper in which these auctions are advertised. Alternatively, most counties maintain a service that picks up such notices and mails you a list of them. Sometimes, however, this service tends to be expensive.

Finding out about the sales is therefore relatively easy, but locating the property to be sold can be difficult because only legal descriptions are provided. As noted in Chapter 3, these do not include a street address. It helps to have a friend in a title insurance company who can supply you with usable addresses from legal descriptions. (See Chapters 3 and 4 for other clues on locating the property.)

Do I Check Out the Property?

Once you've gotten the address, you must take a look at the property because the public notice does not normally give its value, condition, or title status. You must determine the property's condition and worth either by using your own judgment or by using expert help (see Chapter 15 for insights here). You also need to determine whether there's an occupancy problem.

Sometimes the original borrower-owner is still living in the property. If that's the case, you must determine if the trustee or lender will remove the occupant prior to sale or if that occupant has any rights to remain in the property after the sale. A former borrower-seller can turn into a belligerent tenant who can only be removed by eviction. Even this can be problematic if the person has occupancy rights during a redemption period, as may be the case under judicial foreclosure, particularly in some agricultural states.

What Do I Look Out for in Liens and Encumbrances?

The single biggest difficulty in dealing with foreclosure auctions, however, is mistaking which mortgage you're bidding on. You could examine the house, determine that it's worth $100,000, and at the sale find out that the mortgage is only $10,000. So you happily bid $10,000 and are successful. You think you've just bought a house worth $100,000 for $10,000. However, it turns out that there are $90,000 worth of superior mortgages on the property, so in reality you've just bought a house that's no bargain.

TIP

The rule to remember is that any mortgages or other liens recorded *prior* to the mortgage that is foreclosing are not affected by the auction but remain on the property. These are called *superior liens*. Any mortgages or liens (with the possible exception of federal tax liens) recorded after the mortgage that is foreclosing are generally wiped out (extinguished) at the auction. These are called *junior liens*. See the Appendix for more information.

Tax liens are a special problem. Generally speaking, if they are junior (recorded after the mortgage is in foreclosure), the process wipes them out (from the property, not from the seller who may still remain personally liable for the debt). If they were recorded prior, however, they remain in effect, and you will need to pay them off to remove them.

Federal tax liens are somewhat different because federal law supersedes state law. With a federal tax lien, even if junior, the government may have a right of redemption for up to 4 months (and sometimes longer).

Should I Buy Title Insurance?

Yes, by all means. This is really your best title protection. Be aware, however, that most title companies will not usually sell title insurance on properties sold at auction until all redemption periods have cleared.

TRAP

If the borrower filed for bankruptcy, chances are the bankruptcy court stayed the auction of the property pending disposition of the suit. However, the lender may have pleaded that the asset was wasting, and the stay may have been lifted. Be aware that bankruptcy is handled at the federal court, whereas foreclosures are handled at the state level (or privately as with a trust deed). This means that even after you buy the property at auction, the federal court may deem that it did not sell for close enough to market value, and it may set aside the sale. Yes, this is probably a remote possibility, but it's something else to consider.

How Do I Protect Myself against Hidden Liens?

Ultimately, there is no way to guarantee that there won't be any hidden mortgages, tax liens, or similar problems on the property. However, there are some steps you can take to protect yourself.

Read the Mortgage

The mortgage document or the trust deed itself is probably recorded, and you may be able to obtain a copy through a title insurance company. You can also ask the borrower-owner to see a copy, if they kept theirs. The trustee may also have a copy.

Be wary of what you read, however. You may still not know whether the mortgage is a first, second, third, or another just by examining it. Although in recent years many title insurance companies have taken to writing, for example, "this is a secondary lien" on the face of the mortgage, lest anyone be uncertain, that's not a rule cast in stone. The mortgage may not specify that it's a second, first, or whatever.

Sometimes you can directly ask, "Are there any other mortgages or liens on the property?" Ask this of the borrower-seller if they are willing to talk with you. Ask the trustee. Ask any attorneys or agents who are involved in the sale. It couldn't hurt.

Search the Title

This can be done fairly quickly, but it can be expensive. However, if you're a client of a title insurance company, you can sometimes get a preliminary title search (or "prelim") done for free. The prelim should show liens against the property currently of record.

Some investors rely entirely on the prelim, feeling that if it's clear, they have nothing to worry about. Most of the time, they're probably right. But sometimes things do slip through. After all, the title company does not back the prelim. It's only a statement of opinion.

Find Out about Redemption Equities

As noted earlier, in most cases of judicial foreclosure there is also an "equity of redemption." This means the former owner-borrower can redeem the property for a set time after the sale is completed. (In some states this time is a year or longer.)

In other words, if you are in a state that has only judicial foreclosure and you buy a property through a foreclosure sale, it may be that even after you have title, the former owner still has a claim on the property; once having paid back all your foreclosure costs plus interest, the person could demand the property. This potential claim could prevent you from reselling, refinancing, or otherwise dealing with the property.

In addition, as previously noted, there may be a tax redemption period. Be sure you check this out if you find a tax lien on the property.

Determine Your Maximum Bid

Based on your analysis of the property, the title, its condition and how much it will cost to fix it up, how much it's market value is, what your profit will be, and any other factors of influence, determine what your maximum bid will be. Then never bid above that amount.

I can still remember my first auction when I and another person were the last remaining bidders on the property. I was determined to get it. But the other bidder was more determined. I even went a bit above my maximum bid in the heat of the contest. Fortunately, I cooled down and stopped bidding.

The other person got the property for more than I thought it was worth. When I met her a few months later, she bemoaned the fact that she had outbid me. Her costs proved more than anticipated, and instead of a profit, it had turned into a loss.

Remember, the goal is to get a property at a bargain, not to win the bidding at all costs.

Check with an Agent and Attorney

Sometimes you don't have to do much investigating at all. Agents and attorneys who specialize in foreclosure auctions usually keep up on most of the sales. Locate one of these agents or attorneys and give them a call. Right over the phone they may be able to tell you, "That property's so encumbered it isn't even worth considering!" Or, "You won't be alone in bidding because a lot of other investors have seen what a good deal it is."

One phone call to the right person can give you a lot of insight.

TIP

If a superior mortgage is foreclosing, prior to the auction find out if there are junior mortgages. If there are, to protect their position (remember, junior mortgages are wiped out in the auction sale), the lender will need to reinstate the superior mortgage, then add the costs of doing so to its junior mortgage, and start its own foreclosure procedures. However, these junior mortgages are often held by former owners of the property who took back the mortgage as part of a previous sale. They may not know what to do, when to do it, or how. They may be planning on doing nothing and letting their junior mortgage be wiped out by the sale. Contact these people and see if they are willing to sell you the junior mortgages for, as an example, 50 cents on the dollar. If they are, you can then take over the process, carry it out, and get the property at a bargain price. Remember, you'd be doing them a favor because they otherwise might get nothing for their mortgage.

How Do I Arrange Financing?

As noted earlier, cash talks loudest. However, a line of credit from a bank will do just as well.

If neither of these are feasible, check with the trustee. Perhaps the lender who is foreclosing will be willing to arrange financing. If it's a bank, you may be able to fill out an application and receive approval prior to the auction sale. Then, at the sale you can bid the amount of your financing (plus whatever cash you want to invest). You might get the property for 10 percent down or less.

In some cases the trustee will allow a certain period of time, typically 30 days, for the successful bidder to arrange outside financing. This is usually enough time if you're preapproved with a lender. However, keep in mind that if you cannot subsequently get financing, you'll probably lose the cash deposit required for your bid.

TRAP

Keep in mind that for outside financing (from a bank or other lending institution), not only do you have to qualify, but the property must do so as well. If it doesn't appraise for enough, or if there are defects (such as a bad roof) that the lender demands be fixed, you could fail to get financing even if you are preapproved. (Or you might have to come up with the fix-it money yourself.) This could cost you the purchase and your deposit.

How Do I Bid at the Sale?

It's elementary. You just show up and bid. Of course, you must have cash, a cashier's check, or other cash equivalent for the required minimum amount that's been set by the trustee, often 5 percent.

Usually, people will arrive half an hour before the auction at the appropriate spot. If it's a trustee's auction, the trustee (or a designate) will be handling the sale. If it's a mortgage, a judge or a referee may be handling it.

Look around the room. Usually, there will be a fairly large group of people. Don't assume they are all bidders. Some may be gawkers who are curious to see what's going to happen.

Usually, if there are junior mortgages on the property that have not already started foreclosure, the lenders will be there to bid up to their interest in the property to protect it. But sometimes not.

TIP

In an auction, all of the money realized first goes to pay off the foreclosing mortgage plus costs. If any is left, that amount goes to pay the next junior lien. Any more left over goes to pay a subsequent junior lien. Any left after that goes back to the original borrower-owner.

If it looks like this is a good property—in other words, if the mortgage amount is below market value and there are no superior liens—there may be a crowd of bargain seekers, your direct competitors. Don't let them intimidate you.

At the Auction

When it's time for the sale, the referee, trustee, or other person conducting will ask for everyone's attention. This person may be in a corner of a room in an office building or literally on the courthouse steps. Usually, there is no gavel, no shouting, and none of the drama that Hollywood would lead you to expect.

The trustee usually begins by giving both the street address and the legal description of the property. (The legal description is how it's identified in the assessor's and recorder's office and may refer to townships, metes and bounds, or other arcane descriptions.)

Then the person conducting the sale (whom we'll call the trustee) will open any bids received prior to the auction. Usually, there's one bid, which is the lender's, that includes the unpaid balance on the mortgage plus unpaid interest plus costs. (This is sometimes referred to as the *upset amount*.)

The trustee may then open other bids that have been delivered by mail, which can boost the price up. Note: Some auctions are by sealed bid only.

TIP

 To bid at an auction, whether by sealed bid or verbally, you will often be asked to register and provide evidence (in the form of cash, cashier's check, etc.) that you have the wherewithal to make the required deposit should you be the successful bidder.

In a verbal auction, after all written bids are opened and read, the trustee will ask those in attendance if there are any other bids. This is your cue to go into action (presuming you haven't already sent your maximum bid in written form).

At this point members of the audience may begin bidding. Typically, the bidding will start big and end small. By that I mean it may initially jump up in $10,000 increments, then in $1000 increments, and finally end with those bidding up by only $100 increments or less.

Sometimes the bidding can get exciting, with members of the audience urging others to bid higher or, if they're competitors, to bid lower or to stop bidding. Usually, however, it's a fairly quiet and quick process. Within a few minutes, you'll know whether or not you're the highest bidder.

TRAP

At times some nastiness will go on. In some cases the bidding gets fierce and frantic, and it isn't always friendly or entirely on the up and up. For example, several bidders may get together to bid up the price until you and others become disgusted and leave, at which time they withdraw their bids back down to a lower price they had agreed on earlier. There are other nasty tricks as well. It's up to the trustee handling the auction to deal with this. (Sometimes, particularly if there's a registration and cash deposit on hand, the trustee will accept the highest bid and refuse to let it be withdrawn.)

TIP

Don't be intimidated. At my first auction, people were sending in bids right and left. There didn't seem to be time to get my own in. Just stand up and give your name and the amount you bid. Be sure that the trustee or referee hears you and notes what you've said.

What If I Win?

If you're the high bidder, the property is now yours, provided you can pay for it.

As noted, in the case of some trustees, you'll be required to come up with cash immediately. In other cases you'll have some time, typically 30 days, to come up with the balance of the money. See our previous discussion on financing as well as Chapters 16 and 17 for tips here.

Normally, once you're the winning bidder and you've arranged for financing, things play out smoothly, but there are exceptions. It may turn out that there's a cloud on the title (something affecting the ability of the trustee or court to convey clear title to you). Usually that's taken care of prior to the sale, but not always. If that's the case, the sale may be delayed a few weeks or even a month or more to clear the title.

What Should I Do Once I'm the Winner?

Here are some suggestions about what you'll want to do:

- Arrange for the financing if you haven't already done so.
- Get fire and liability insurance on the property right away. (You may want to arrange for this to go into effect the moment it's yours.) Often, these properties are vacant, and vandalism can take its toll.

- Get title insurance. This doesn't guarantee clear title to you, but it does mean that the title insurance company will defend your title up to the amount of the insurance.

- Protect the property. You'll want to board it up, put a fence around, put a guard on it, or whatever to be sure that no new damage is done.

- Remove the old borrower-owner or tenant if they are in possession. This may require the use of an *unlawful detainer* action (eviction) and could take as long as a month or more.

- Do whatever else is necessary to protect your property and title.

TRAP

If you are the successful bidder and it turns out you can't get financing or for some other reason can't come up with the cash to close the deal, you'll probably lose your deposit. Keep in mind that unlike conventional real estate transactions, where there's a contingency clause in the purchase agreement that specifies if you can't get financing the deal is off and you get your money back, no such clause is likely to be in effect here. At an auction it's either put up or lose. It's one of the risks you take to buy a bargain property.

Is It Worth It?

Bargains—very big bargains—do exist at foreclosure auctions. These big bargains, however, are offset by the risks, many of which we've discussed here. It basically comes down to putting up your money and taking your chances, tempered by all the investigation and research you can do.

My advice is that before you jump into the arena of foreclosure auctions, you find an expert in the field to help you get started. This can be an experienced real estate broker, an attorney, or even another investor. Watch this person operate first with their (or someone else's) money. See how it's done. Then have them help you with your first bidding action.

In addition get lots of money, more than you calculate you'll need. There are almost always more expenses than we anticipate. When dealing with auctions, where there are definite time limits for producing the cash, you don't want to be a dollar short or a day late.

Perhaps most important of all, be aware of the risk of buying blindly. Remember in spite of your best research, you might think you're buying a first mortgage when in reality it's only a third. As with most things, when the rewards go up, so do the risks. This is an area for hardy risk takers.

At foreclosure auctions properties are frequently sold for a small fraction of their market value. It's a very tempting area of real estate to get into.

12

Buying at Probate and Tax Sales

For those who like a challenge, bargain opportunities abound in a wide variety of forced sales. Here it is frequently possible to purchase a property for a fraction of its market value. The beauty of these sales is that they are held frequently in many communities around the country. If you want to look for bargains in forced sales, chances are that one is being held somewhere near you this week.

Most forced sales involve cash, but this is not always the case. Frequently, the property being disposed of will be subject to existing mortgages, which in essence means that you only need the down payment. In many cases it is possible to arrange outside financing in advance for 90 percent or more of the purchase price. (Check Chapter 16 to see how to raise 100 percent of the financing.)

What Are Forced Sales?

A forced sale is essentially a liquidation. For one reason or another, a property owner wants to cash out. That property is therefore put on the auction block and goes to the highest bidder.

Properties at forced sales almost always sell for less than market value and sometimes for considerably less. There's a good reason for this.

Consider a homebuyer looking to purchase a house. The buyer probably contacts a number of agents and goes to see the houses listed. The houses are open for inspection. Often, they have been prettied up.

When the buyer selects one to purchase, the purchase is handled in a civilized fashion. An offer is made and negotiations commence. One or more agents work with the buyer to consummate the deal. Soon a deal may be struck. Once the papers are signed, the buyer knows the house is tied up. Assuming the deal was properly worded, the buyer usually has 30 to 60 days to secure financing; if proper financing can't be obtained, the buyer can back out without losing a dime.

On the other hand, consider the case of a forced sale. Inspecting the property may be difficult. It may be necessary to phone an executor or administrator and have that person take time off from work to come out and show the property, which may prove to be neglected and in disrepair.

A buyer who wishes to purchase it must then usually show up before a judge or magistrate and publicly bid for the property with other buyers. Often, the buyer must immediately come up with a 5 or 10 percent cash deposit. Instead of a long escrow, anywhere from no time at all to 30 days may be allowed to raise the full price—in cash. And if the buyer can't find proper financing, however earnestly having sought it, then he or she may lose the entire deposit!

As a result few people are inclined to become involved in forced sales. Very rarely will a homebuyer bid. And because of the hassle involved, relatively few investors bid either. Consequently, the only people who usually show up are bargain hunters. And they, as we all know, aren't going to be willing to pay anywhere near market price. Hence, properties that sell at forced sales usually go for below market—sometimes far below market. There are bargains to be had here.

A variety of forced sales are available. Principal among these are probate sales and tax sales. Each is handled a bit differently than the others.

Probate Sales

Probate is the American way of disposing of property upon an individual's death. It arises out of British common law, and in theory its purpose is to see that all interested parties have the opportunity to present their lawful claims and have them paid from the dead person's estate.

In practice this means that probate allows all creditors to be paid off. In essence, therefore, probate is the legal means that creditors have of collecting debts after a person dies.

The problems and drawbacks of probate are legendary. Anyone who has ever been an heir and seen the deceased's estate scooped out to pay creditors, enormous probate attorney fees, and other costs must surely dread the whole process. (There are several ways of avoiding probate, including living trusts and changing the way that title to property is held, and you'd do well to check with your attorney.)

Because of the need to raise cash to pay off creditors and to pay the hefty attorney fees, those handling probates must often sell the deceased's real estate. Thus, we have the "probate sale."

TIP

The person handling the sale is either the administrator or the executor. An *administrator* is a court-appointed fiduciary; an *executor* is a fiduciary nominated in a will and approved by the court.

Selling Property in Probate

An administrator is frequently an attorney. An executor may be either an attorney or a layperson. In either case it frequently becomes their responsibility to dispose of real estate. For example, we'll say that Joseph died several months ago. Since he didn't leave a will (died intestate), an administrator has been appointed by the court to handle the probate.

Joe left behind a four-bedroom, two-bathroom house. The house has been sitting vacant, and the estate has been paying the mortgage on it. Since the estate needs money (to pay creditors and attorney fees), the administrator has decided to sell the house.

The administrator has several options here. She can list the house with a real estate agent. She can try to sell it herself on the open market, sort of "by owner" (the estate theoretically owns the house, but the administrator runs the estate). Or she can phone an investor friend of hers and ask him if he might want to buy it. The administrator in theory can even buy the property herself, but that is unlikely because it could be construed as a conflict of interest. (The administrator or executor is responsible for getting the best deal for the estate.)

Regardless of what course the administrator or executor selects, the sale must be approved by the court. Let's follow through to see how this works.

Following through on a Probate Sale

We'll say that the administrator or executor decides to go as public as possible and lists the property with a real estate agent; thus, the property will probably appear on the multiple-listing service of the local real estate board. The house will probably have a sign posted, and it may even be advertised; in addition there will be a listed price.

I recently observed a probate sale handled in this fashion not far from where I live. The houses in the area had a market value of $150,000. The probate house was listed for $115,000. Needless to say, it caused quite a stir.

Probate property must be appraised; the price usually can be no less than 90 percent of appraisal. But such appraisals are often notoriously low. Soon there were 11 offers on the property.

The executor received all the offers but could not accept any of them. In a probate sale, only the court can accept an offer. The executor set a date on which all the offers were to be presented to the court.

At the appointed time and place at the county courthouse, a magistrate (sometimes called a referee) brought up the matter of the probate sale. The executor dutifully presented all 11 offers. They ranged from a low of $105,000 to a high of $118,000. (Several people had bid more than the asking price!)

The magistrate examined the offers to be sure they were legitimate (filled out sales offer, with an appropriate deposit in the form of a cashier's check) and then took the highest bid (called the upset price), saying, "I'm opening the bidding at $118,000. Will anyone bid higher?"

All of the people who had made offers (or their representatives) could now raise their bids. In addition anyone at all who came into the courtroom and could establish credentials as a legitimate bidder (by having 5 percent of the bid price in a cashier's check) could also bid.

The bidding started and moved up by thousands of dollars, then by hundreds, and then by fifties. The highest final bid was $129,850. The magistrate sold the house to that person, an individual who hadn't even bothered earlier to submit an offer to the executor.

Note two important points. First, making a written offer to an executor or administrator may not amount to a hill of beans in a probate sale. It is showing up at the sale and bidding that usually takes priority. Second, even though there was strong competition in this case, the final price was still a bargain, probably more than $20,000 below market value.

Finding Out about Probate Sales

In our example the administrator took the most public means of letting people know about the sale. Finding out about probates like these is easy. Just contact any broker.

Unfortunately, sales such as this tend to be the exception. More often than not, I have seen executors and administrators "vest-pocket" the sale, which means that they pretty much kept it to themselves. Of course, they can't keep the sale entirely quiet because the court could accuse them of impropriety or conflict of interest and dismiss them. But in most cases the administrator or executor will do only the minimum necessary. This usually means advertising the property to be sold in a legal paper. The ad need not be enticing, nor might the paper it is published in have a wide circulation. Nevertheless, it's enough for the watchful bargain hunter.

If you watch a legal newspaper closely, you should see advertisements for probate sales crop up. Even if you don't see advertisements for real estate sales themselves, notices of probate most certainly will appear (giving creditors notice that they have only a limited time in which to make their claims). Since there frequently is real estate to be sold, simply calling the administrator or executor anytime you see a probate notice should result in a fair number of opportunities to bid on properties.

Remember, regardless of how close to the vest an administrator wants to handle the disposal of real property, at some point advertising will probably occur. And even if the administrator won't accept an offer from you, you can almost always show up at the sale and make your bid along with everyone else.

Financing and the Probate Sale

Death does not wipe out a mortgage. Thus, if I own mortgaged property and die and that property is sold through probate, the mortgage continues in force. If you buy that property, you therefore buy it subject to the mortgage.

This is an important concept. You may be bidding on a property at the $100,000 level, but there may be a $70,000 mortgage on it. Thus, the most the estate can hope to receive is $30,000.

By finding out about the probate property well in advance, you can contact the lender and see if you can assume the mortgage. If you can, then you need to come up with only $30,000 instead of $100,000.

If you don't have sufficient cash to pay off the mortgage, then perhaps you can make arrangements with a bank, savings and loan, or mortgage banker to prefinance your purchase. You'll have to qualify as to credit. And you'll probably want to have an appraiser qualify the property. Once you have done these two things, a lender should be willing to give you a firm loan commitment; for example, 90 percent of your purchase price up to a maximum amount. Now when you bid, you need come up with substantially less.

Alternatively, the estate can sometimes agree to handle the financing itself. Perhaps instead of cash, the estate wants a long-term mortgage that it can give to the heirs. Perhaps the estate is willing to offer 80 percent financing to you if you have proper credit.

You would need to negotiate with the administrator about this. And you'd be unlikely to get court approval for overly favorable terms unless the price you paid was closer to market value. Nevertheless, in this fashion you could arrange financing whereby you didn't need to qualify or pay loan fees.

Getting Started

Get a copy of your local legal paper. Look for advertisements for services that cover probates; sometimes there are services that, for a fee, will provide you with detailed information well in advance on probate sales. If there are no services, check the paper for probates and probate sales. Also check with your real estate broker for any listed probate properties.

Investigate. Call the executor or administrator. This is just a person like you or me, one who will probably (though not always) be delighted to receive your call. Get as much information as you can. Look at the property. Evaluate it. Go to your bank and arrange for the financing. Show up on auction day. Bid! You too can purchase probate property.

Pitfalls

There are tricks to auctions. You will want to be sure you know about all the loans on the property. Check the title on the property first. Insist on a title report and title insurance from the selling estate as a condition of your purchase.

Check the property's condition and occupancy. Sometimes these properties stand neglected for months and can have considerable damage. In other cases they are rented out. Sometimes relatives are living in them. Be sure you know that you can get any residents out.

Take a dry run first. Probate sales are complex financial purchases. The first time do everything as if you were going to bid and purchase, but instead of opening your mouth, just stand and watch. You can learn an enormous amount.

Tax Sales

Tax sales involve taking a property away from its owner by force and selling it on the courthouse steps to the highest bidder to raise money to satisfy a tax debt.

Property Tax Sales

Each county and state collects property taxes. (Actually, the counties collect the taxes, but much of the money is then forwarded to the state for distribution.) The property taxes become a lien on real estate and are due at a certain date each year. (In California, for example, the first installment is due on December 10, and the second on April 10.) If the taxes are not paid by a deadline date, then the property is sold to the state. (For information on IRS tax sales, see Chapter 8.)

The state usually allows a long period of redemption (5 years in California and in many other states). During that time the owner can redeem the property by paying the back taxes and penalties.

Property taxes are a priority lien; they come before any mortgages. This means that once the property is sold to the state, any mortgages on it are normally wiped out. Virtually all mortgages (and trust deeds) therefore contain clauses that allow the lender to pay the delinquent taxes, add the money thus spent to the mortgage, and foreclose. This is for the lender's protection.

Thus, most properties sold to the state for back taxes and not subsequently redeemed are free and clear (that is, the mortgage lender did not pay the taxes to bail out the property). These properties are usually improved lots and older, smaller homes.

Those properties taken back by the counties are usually sold to the public once or twice a year at tax lien sales. The property goes to the highest bidder. Lots valued at $1000 might sometimes sell for $100, and homes can sell for a quarter of their value. Because the state really doesn't care about getting market price and because few people know about and attend these sales, there are some real bargains available.

The successful bidder gets a "tax deed," which is normally sufficient to get title insurance.

How to Take Advantage of Property Tax Sales.   To find out about tax sales, you must contact the appropriate person in each county or township. That could be the county assessor, tax collector, recorder, or other person whose duties are to handle the sale. This person will provide you with a list of properties and the time of the sale.

As a bidder, it is your responsibility to:

1. Inspect the property and determine its condition. (Properties are usually sold "as is.")
2. Get your own title report and title insurance.
3. Secure your own prefinancing.
4. Determine the property's true value and how much you are willing to pay.

Then it's more or less like the other sales. You show up at the time of the sale, have the stated minimum deposit either in cash or in a cashier's check, and bid on the property.

If you've done your homework, found a good property, made sure of its condition and financing, and bid an appropriate amount, you could just have made the bargain investment of your life!

The Bottom Line

Forced sales can offer big profits to the bargain hunter. But they're not for everyone. They are for those who are careful, who arrange their financing in advance, who check out the properties, and who are willing to take the risks.

13
Buying "As Is"

If you've looked around at any bargain properties, whether they be from HUD, Fannie Mae, or from a private seller, very likely you've run into the expression "as is." This is pretty much standard usage in the paperwork on the sale of REOs and other bargain real estate. It's vitally important that you know what this term really means and how it can affect your investment.

"As is" means without warranty. The seller is not warrantying the condition of the property. You're being given fair warning that if there's a problem, it's up to you to solve it. In other words, don't come crying back to the seller later on.

But of course, it's not that simple (life seldom is). Sellers are supposed to disclose to you any defects. Selling "as is" does not usually relieve them of this responsibility. At least that's the case when the seller is an individual. For example, if the house has a leaky roof, the seller may disclose that fact to you and then offer to sell "as is." If you buy, you acknowledge that you know about the roof and agree to accept the property in its current condition. You understand that the seller is not going to be responsible for fixing that roof.

However, if you buy the house and later discover that the plumbing is plugged and that the seller knew about it and didn't disclose that fact to you, even if you bought "as is," you may have good grounds for demanding the seller fix the plumbing problem because it wasn't disclosed.

Notice that "as is" does not normally remove the seller's responsibility for disclosure. It only removes the seller's warranty with regard to fixing.

TIP

Property sold "as is" is considered to have raised a warning flag. Presumably, sellers wouldn't sell in this fashion unless there was a problem. Hence, buyers normally assume, in conventional real estate sales, that when property is sold "as is," there's something wrong with it. Therefore, to make the sale, sellers must usually sell below market. As a result "as is" often means bargain!

When the Seller Is a Company or Organization

However, when the seller of an REO is a bank (nationally chartered so federal laws supersede state statutes), HUD, Freddie Mac, or some other giant entity, other rules tend to apply. REOs offered for sale "as is" by these giants often come without full disclosures.

In other words, the seller may not tell you what's wrong with the property. After the sale, if you discover a leaky roof or bad plumbing and you complain, you will be shown the "as is" clause and told that you really are on your own.

TIP

When buying an REO "as is," because there may not be full disclosure and because the property is sold without warranty, you really need to do a thorough job of inspecting it (see Chapter 15).

Why Do Large Sellers Not Give Full Disclosure?

The reason that big REO sellers seldom give full disclosure about their properties is that, while the seller may be the owner of record, the company organization almost certainly never lived in the property. Therefore, no one in the seller's office actually knows its true condition. You can't honestly disclose what you don't know.

But, you may reasonably ask, why doesn't the seller conduct an inspection and give disclosures based on it? The answer is that in fact this is often done. These large sellers have their own inspectors who check out properties. When defects of a serious nature are found, they are duly noted and usually, but not always, reported to the buyer.

However, as we'll see in Chapter 15 on inspections, you can't easily detect what you can't see. There may be hidden defects that an REO seller would have no knowledge of even with an inspection. (On the other hand, an owner who actually lives in the property may have ready knowledge of the problems.) Hence, there is an overall lack of disclosures.

Many states that require disclosures from sellers may offer exemptions for REO sellers. And as noted earlier, federal law preempts state law, and these large REO sellers as a result may not be subject to the usual disclosures requirements.

TIP

Federal rules do require some disclosures. For example, the seller must usually disclose knowledge of lead paint in the property, and the buyer has 10 days to withdraw from the sale. However, again, these rules do not always seem to apply when the seller is a national or quasi-government organization.

Why Do Large Sellers Insist on Selling "As Is"?

These sellers usually want to be out of the property completely after the sale. Remember, they've already taken the property back once. Until they sell it, it's on their books as a liability. They don't want to have to deal with it as a liability a second time after they've once sold it. They want a final sale. Therefore, they sell "as is" and without warranty so that the buyer has little recourse to come back.

Therefore, when buying an REO, you'd better be quite sure that you know what you're getting. If it later turns out that the property has a problem, you won't easily get the seller to correct it.

Can I Negotiate "As Is" Terms?

One of the first things that investors learn about real estate is that everything is negotiable. Almost everything.

When dealing with these large REO sellers, I've discovered that the one thing they almost universally will not negotiate is the "as is" clause. You are far more likely to get them to spring for some cash to help you fix up the property than you are to get them to warrant its condition. Indeed, if you insist on removing the "as is" clause from the contract, my experience suggests you're most likely to have your offer rejected.

When Must I Inspect the Property?

As noted earlier, this means that the onus is on you, the buyer, to conduct a thorough investigation of the property. However, unlike the purchase of a home in the conventional manner, you typically cannot write an inspection clause into the contract and expect to have it accepted.

TIP

When purchasing residential real estate today, it is very common for the buyer to insist on the right to hire a professional inspector to check out the home. Typically, buyers will demand 2 weeks for the process after the seller accepts the offer. And if the inspection reveals problems, the buyer also typically demands the right to back out of the purchase contract without penalty (no loss of deposit).

Part of the "as is" nature of REO contracts from many (but not all) lenders is that this inspection clause cannot be present in the contract. In other words you do not have the right to back out of the deal after an inspection.

This means that to determine whether the property has problems, you must do your inspection before you make the offer. You will typically be afforded access to the property for this purpose.

However, herein lies a money problem. If you hire an inspector, it can cost you upwards of $250 or more for the 2 or 3 hours the inspector is out there. Most investors would consider this money well spent, provided they ultimately get the property. However, remember that your inspection may need to occur before your offer is accepted. You could easily pay for an inspection, make an offer, and then learn that the property was sold to someone else. At $250 or more a pop, you're not going to want to make a whole lot of these speculative inspections. (We'll have some suggestions on how to get around this in Chapter 15.)

Buying "as is" increases the risk to you, the buyer. Hence, you should build in a reduced bargain price to justify doing it.

14
After Natural Calamities

Shakespeare wrote in *Henry IV,* "the ill wind which blows no man to good."

We live in an era of increased threat from natural catastrophes. Whatever the cause, whether it be from global warming, sunspots, the anger of our ancestors, or whatever, the last decade has seen more flooding, fires, hurricanes, and other natural calamities than any decade of the previous 150 years. In short the times are increasingly challenging.

Answering that challenge can provide opportunities for those looking for hidden real estate bargains.

Where's the Opportunity?

Almost anytime a natural calamity occurs, real estate prices in the area take a nosedive. Whether it's an earthquake in California, a hurricane off the East Coast, or floods in the Midwest, there are people who decide they simply don't want to take any more. They put their property up for sale, and they move on. When fire swept through the hilly parts of Oakland, California, in the early 1990s, real estate prices fell 30 to 50 percent in 15 days.

Because of the number of these properties suddenly offered and because of the uncertainties of the times, sellers can't find buyers. And prices drop. When this occurs, it can be a rare bargain opportunity for investors.

TIP

There's an old saying that goes, "If you can keep your head when everyone else is losing theirs, you simply don't understand the situation!" It's true. But perhaps the reason you aren't caught up in the panic of the moment is because you have a longer term perspective.

Six months after that fire in Oakland, California, prices were not only back up to where they were previously, but they were 10 percent higher!

It's important to understand that I'm not advocating taking advantage of someone else's misery. I'm not suggesting that you look for someone who is forced to sell and then undercut them with a low price. The Federal Emergency Management Association (FEMA), the Red Cross, and other agencies are available to help such people regroup, salvage what they can, and rebuild on their property.

Rather, I'm suggesting that every time there's a disaster, there are a good number of people who decide to pack up and move elsewhere. This is commonly seen after every earthquake in California, when large numbers of people leave their homes and go to the unshaking ground of the East Coast. It is also seen when those on the East Coast, after a hurricane, pack up and leave for the calmer winds of California.

In addition there are those who simply do not want to rebuild. They'd rather take what insurance money they are offered, sell for whatever they can get, and then buy a ready-to-go property in a nearby but unaffected area.

There's no stopping those who flee. Yet, there is an opportunity to help them do what they want by purchasing their properties at the going market rate. At the moment that rate is typically lower than before, and often later, than the event.

Is This a Risky Investment?

I would definitely classify it as risky. There are two major elements to the risk. The first is that you never know if the area is actually going to come back to where it was before. Ten years after the 1989 earthquake in the San Fernando Valley of California, there were still many boarded up properties that had never been refurbished, never cleaned up, and never brought back to their former condition. And in those areas, prices likewise had not yet moved back. There's no guarantee that after a large natural disaster, the area will rejuvenate. It could plateau at a lower economic level and lower market values.

The second risk is not knowing what may be required to fix up a property. For example, after the Oakland fires noted earlier, I looked at many of the homes in the area that had been damaged. Some needed to be bull-dozed and new homes erected. Others required rebuilding.

Who could determine what the costs would be? Would the local building department determine that an old foundation was sound? Or would it demand that it be removed and repoured? Would old structures that were built to a building code of 70 years earlier be allowed to remain and be fixed? Or would they need to be torn down?

In addition it's one thing to get a professional to look at a job and give you an estimate when there's only one house that needs work. But what about when there are a thousand? Building contractors were taking appointments months in advance just to come out and give a bid. Yet, in order to buy, you had to make an offer now.

Thus, there are big risks investing in bargain real estate after a natural disaster. You don't know for sure that prices will come back up. You can't accurately determine what your costs will be. That in fact is the very reason that the prices are driven so low.

TIP

Remember, you're not taking advantage of someone who wants to sell. You're shifting their risk onto your back for a chance at a big profit.

On the other hand, most areas do bounce back. In fact many come back even stronger because the properties now are all new and usually fancier than before.

How Do I Determine If an Area Is Likely to Bounce Back?

There is no way to know for sure, but there are at least three factors to consider:

- **Is there a strong economic base?** When a volcano ravaged the big island of Hawaii a few years ago, a large number of homes were destroyed. However, that didn't keep tourists, the big source of income, from visiting. (Some came during the eruptions just to seem them.) You have to look closely at an area. Were the factories and office buildings that create the economic base destroyed or only the housing? If it's only the housing, that economic base is going to demand quick rebuilding.

- **Is there a large or small supply of housing?** In parts of the Northeast and Midwest, some cities have a surplus of housing. Homes go unsold for 6 months or more because there are no buyers. In short the area is overbuilt for the working population. If a natural disaster were to wipe out a portion of the housing market, it might just bring it in line with the demand. Thus, after an initial dump in prices for reasons we saw earlier, there might be no bounce back. You have to assess the supply and demand of housing in the area. If the supply is short, it is almost certain a significant bump in prices will soon be forthcoming. If the supply is huge, there may be no bump at all.

- **Is there high morale in the populace?** Check the newspapers. Are civic leaders wringing their hands and moaning? Or are they on their soapboxes promising a new and revitalized area? After the initial shock is over, are companies pouring money into the area to build new plants with more jobs? Or are they shunning the location. In short is the area seen as a pariah or as a focus of opportunity?

The remaining factor is how willing you are to take this sort of risk. As I noted in the beginning, it's hard to keep your cool when everyone is running around saying the sky is falling.

However, I have found that those who bet against the vitality of local communities in this country, who bet that prices will stay down instead of rise, have usually been the losers. Those who bet on a brighter future are most often the winners.

15

How to Inspect a Bargain Property

Whenever you buy any property, you should have it inspected. However, when you are buying a bargain property, you should probably have it inspected twice. That's because very often the reason it's a bargain is that there's something wrong with it. You want to know exactly what that something is, how much it will cost to fix, or if it can be fixed at all. In fact your inspection may determine whether you make an offer or walk away.

When inspecting bargain properties, you actually need to make three separate inspections. Inspect:

- The neighborhood
- The physical condition of the property
- The title

What Should I Look for in the Neighborhood?

We all know what a great neighborhood looks like. The streets are wide, the lawns and gardens are all manicured, the houses are brightly painted—it just looks good. If the house you're considering is in a neighborhood like this, you probably don't need to look much further.

However, most of the time you'll be looking at properties in poorer quality neighborhoods. The question becomes: Just how bad is it?

TRAP

 Beware of REO slums. This seems to be particularly the case with HUD properties. Sometimes developers will sell all their homes on FHA loans. Later, for whatever reason, a large percentage of the owners default, and HUD takes the properties back. As a result in some neighborhoods, every other home is a HUD repo. And with so many vacant properties, the neighborhood quickly deteriorates. Gangs pervade the area, and sometimes these homes are vandalized and become crack houses. No matter how good a deal you get on a property in an REO slum, it's probably not worthwhile because it will take a massive effort to turn the area around, and one homeowner can't do it alone. Fixing up your house will be like dropping money down a bottomless pit. The poor neighborhood will keep you from renting it out at a good rate or selling for a profit.

Check the quality of surrounding homes. Hopefully, if they do not have manicured lawns, the landscaping is in fairly good shape. Although the homes may not have been painted recently, they should still look fairly clean.

Check carefully to see that the surrounding homes (both on the street of your subject home and nearby streets) are occupied. An occasional empty house with a For Rent or For Sale sign is not a problem. But houses that are abandoned can be. They can become a focus for crime and vandalism.

TIP

 Look for graffiti on fences and walls. In our modern world, graffiti occur almost everywhere. But in a strong neighborhood, homeowners will quickly get out there and paint over graffiti. In a weak neighborhood, graffiti will remain to encourage vandalism and gang activities.

Also look for the amenities that a good neighborhood offers. Are there nearby parks that are clean without vagrants sleeping in them? Is there nearby shopping? What about easy access to freeways and mass transit? Is it close to employment centers?

Pay particular attention to schools. The quality of schools is the most important factor in determining the quality of the neighborhood. Stop by local schools and ask to see their test scores. These are available to the public. Explain that you're thinking of buying a home in the area.

You don't need to have scores in the 90th percentile (though if you do, that's wonderful). However, scores in the 20th percentile are not good. Families will shun these schools, opting for neighborhoods with better schools, making it more difficult to rent and/or sell.

Also check for crime in the area. Visit the local police station. Their community affairs officer should be more than happy to let you see crime statistics by neighborhood and block. Stay away from high-crime areas. You could get hit while fixing up the property, and you will certainly have a more difficult time renting and then selling than in a lower crime area.

You may be thinking that this requires a lot of investigating before even getting to the house. But consider that you're not checking out a single home; you're checking a whole neighborhood. The results of your inspection may cause you to avoid entire blocks, entire neighborhoods, or entire sections of a city. You're doing your homework to be sure you buy a property that will rent well and sell quickly for a good profit.

What Should I Check in the Home Itself?

I suggest that you hire a professional inspector to check out the property. However, if you're familiar with home inspections, then by all means also do a thorough check yourself. You will want to pay particular attention to the following areas.

TIP

You want to know what problems exist because you will probably have to fix them. Although you may be able to purchase the property with the problems (because the seller is helping finance the sale and/or is selling "as is"), you may not be able to rent out the property or later sell it yourself. Remember, you'll have to give full disclosure, and if there's a problem, buyers may be scared away. If there's a big problem, lenders may be scared away too. Don't think you can simply buy and overlook the problems. As short a time as 25 years ago, you might have. But it's unlikely you'll be able to today.

Overall Appearance

Most people can recognize a good-looking house when they see it. The design of the front is appealing. The layout or floor plan works. The house has a kind of homey appeal. On the other hand, some homes just look awkward. It may be the design or the placement on the lot. Remember, first impressions are important. If you don't like it, who else will?

But you'll also want to trust more than intuition. Look for homes that have at least three bedrooms and two baths. Fewer make the home more difficult to rent and sell. Also watch out for huge homes with five or more bedrooms. If your plans include renting, you'll find that you may be obliged to take in large families with many children or even more than one family. And this usually puts extra stress on the property. You want a home that's moderate in size.

Landscaping

A house with good landscaping is a plus. But one where the lawn has gone to weed and the shrubs, bushes, and trees are wild and untrimmed should not be removed from consideration. Actually, the most important aspect of landscaping is how the neighboring homes look. If they are in good shape, the subject home can quickly be brought into shape as well.

For a few thousand dollars, you can add an average-sized lawn (from sod) and landscaping to the front of almost any home. In fact, if done as soon as you take possession of the property, the landscaping can be ready and growing by the time other repair work is completed (which is a good reason to start landscaping first).

Beware, however, of any sinkholes or standing water because it suggests poor drainage, which is a serious problem that can affect the foundation and structure of the house. You may need a soils engineer to evaluate the problem and suggest the cost and means of remedying it.

Exterior

Old and flaky paint, loose boards, torn screens, even broken windows may be the rule. However, these are all cosmetic problems that usually can be quickly, cheaply, and effectively corrected. Most investors I know have a repairperson or two on call or do this work themselves.

There are a number of things you must be wary of. One is lead paint. Prior to 1978, lead paint was commonly used on homes. If the subject home was built prior to that date (or even around that date), suspect lead in the paint.

It costs about $300 to have paint samples analyzed for lead, and this is about the only way you can really tell. But removing the lead paint can easily cost $10,000 or more. Unlike asbestos, for which encasement is usually considered a remedy, lead paint must be removed by a toxic chemical abatement company. (Attempting to remove it yourself by chipping, burning, sanding, or other means usually only releases it into the air or ground causing an even more serious problem.)

TRAP

If you're buying an older home, lead paint may be a serious issue because of the cost of removal. You may want to get an inspection and insist that the seller (REO or other) help pay for the removal. If the seller refuses, you may want to reconsider purchasing the property.

Additionally, be wary of rotted wood. Dry rot or other types of mold can eat through the facing of a home and into the structural boards causing expensive repairs. Usually, you can tell if this is problem because of nail popping, soft and squishy areas in wood siding, or the appearance of black mold.

If you suspect rotted wood, arrange for a pest inspection (available from termite inspectors). This costs a couple of hundred dollars, but it can save you a huge bundle in other unexpected repair costs.

Finally, be on the look out for anything unusual. Stucco separating from the wall suggests serious structural problems. Cracks more than one-sixteenth inch in any masonry should be carefully evaluated. Chimneys that are at an angle or have other problems may need to be replaced (at a cost of thousands).

As I said, if you're not sure, have a professional check it out.

Interior

As with the exterior, most bargain homes are going to need cosmetic repair of the interior. This typically means repainting all of the walls and perhaps the ceilings (depending on what material they are made of). You should also think about replacing or at least cleaning all carpeting.

TIP

Inexpensive yet good-looking carpeting for the average 2000-square-foot home can cost as little as $3000 installed. Professionally painting the entire interior can cost as little $1500.

Also, as noted earlier, watch out for asbestos. This is a tiny fiber that can cause catastrophic health problems when released into the environment. If you're not sure, have a professional check out the property for asbestos-related problems and suggest solutions.

Of greater concern are those items that are not cosmetic such as counters, countertops, tile floors, appliances, sinks, toilets, and so forth. If you get into renovating the home, the costs can skyrocket. For more information on how to evaluate home remodeling as well as estimating costs, I suggest you check my book *Tips and Traps When Renovating Your Home* (McGraw-Hill, 2000).

Basic Systems

These include heating, air conditioning, plumbing (both potable and waste), electrical, and any other system the home may have. These basic systems are often hard to evaluate. If they are broken, it's mandatory that you fix them. And yet, the money spent fixing them never shows up; subsequent buyers simply assume that they all will be in working condition and will not pay a dime more because you spent a fortune getting them in shape.

TRAP

The problem with evaluating basic systems is that sometimes the electricity and water are turned off when you make your inspection of the home. If that's the case, you have no easy way to tell if the heating, air conditioning, plumbing, or electrical are working. If at all possible, try to arrange for an inspection when the utilities are turned on.

Be aware that the older the home, the more likely one of the basic systems is in need of work. Indeed, if you're dealing with a very old home (more than 50 or 60 years), the various systems may be obsolete and need to be replaced.

For example, some older homes have no ground wire installed throughout the property. For safety reasons a ground wire is mandated by all modern building codes. Retrofitting to include a ground may require rewiring the home, a very expensive proposition because it involves breaking into walls and sometimes ceilings and floors. It can cost $5000 or more.

Similarly, in older homes galvanized steel plumbing was frequently used. However, over time calcification and rusting can either clog or rot through these pipes. Small leaks can frequently be fixed. But if the entire system begins to go, it may require extensive replumbing with copper tubing. Again, this is very expensive and can cost upwards of $10,000.

A new forced air heater/air conditioner can easily run $4000 to $5000 installed. A new water heater can cost $400 to $500 installed.

Thus, the various home systems that are not clearly visible can be a serious problem. You should make every effort to have them correctly evaluated before you make your offer.

TIP

In some cases it is possible to buy (for a few hundred dollars) a home warranty plan that will cover most of these systems. However, all home warranty plans I've seen require that the seller warrant that all systems in the house are in good working order at the time of sale. This, unfortunately, is not likely to happen when you buy an REO.

Roof

More problems occur with the roof than with probably any other feature of a home during a sale. Roofs tend to leak, and the same is sometimes true even of newer roofs if they were installed incorrectly.

It goes without saying that you should have a good roof inspection. A roofer will usually do this for you, often for free. However, there are certain signs you can look for yourself.

Check for watermarks in the attic. There should be none. If they exist, it suggests that water is coming through the roof. If they are in just one area, perhaps a patch will do. If they are all over, perhaps the entire roof needs to be replaced.

Look at the roof through a pair of binoculars. Are there any shingles missing? If so, they will most certainly need to be replaced. With any type of clay roof, more important is the fact that the underlayment beneath the missing shingles may have been exposed to the elements and damaged. It's this underlayment, often a type of tarpaper, that actually keeps the water out. Replacing it often requires removal and then replacement of the shingles, which is a costly process.

If the roof is fiberglass-asphalt, are any of the shingle ends curling up? This can happen in very hot climates and suggests that the roof is near the end of its life span.

Also be aware that all roofs wear out eventually. Any roof that is more than 10 years old should be suspect.

Replacing a roof, assuming there is no structural damage, can cost as little as around $5000 for an asphalt shingle or rock-tar roof to well over $20,000 for a tile roof. It's definitely something to consider when inspecting bargain homes.

Foundation

If there's a problem with the foundation, it's time to reevaluate the purchase.

Foundation problems take many forms. With a peripheral foundation (it goes around the outer edge of the house), cracking is usually the biggest concern. When the foundation cracks, the house can literally split from the bottom up. Or it can settle with one side lower than the other.

To check for these cracks, you need to "walk the foundation." Don't worry about tiny cracks (less than one-sixteenth inch wide). These probably don't mean much. But be very wary of larger cracks, particularly the dreaded "V" crack, which is wider at the top than at the bottom. It suggests that the foundation not only has split but that any rebars (reinforcement steel bars) inside may also have split. (Or perhaps the foundation was built without steel reinforcement, which is a worse scenario.)

Look at the bottom of the foundation too. Check to see if the ground underneath has been worn away by water erosion.

If there is a slab (a single piece of concrete forming the floor of the house), check for offsets where it has cracked and part has sunk. Also check for wide cracks. (Again, tiny cracks are not usually a problem.) Often, you can feel these by walking on the floor in stocking feet.

TRAP

 The biggest problem with inspecting the foundation is getting to a place where you can see it. Many times siding or debris will be piled up on the outside of the house making it impossible to view. Other times access under the house may be limited or difficult to get to. And wall-to-wall carpeting can hide a myriad of problems with a slab. The only answer, however, is to move the debris, go where it's hard to go, and pull back the carpeting (with the seller's permission, of course).

Houses with foundation problems usually need creative solutions. The tried and true method of temporarily raising the house on wood beams, breaking out the old foundation, and installing a new one is usually prohibitively expensive, often costing $50,000 and sometimes much more.

Some savvy investors have bought bargain homes for 10 cents on the dollar because of foundation problems and then have used piers sunk into the earth, have injected stratifying substances into the soil underneath, or have used steel to bolt together broken foundation pieces. Many times these investors reap huge profits when their plans succeed.

If you find a house with an identified foundation problem, have a structural engineer and a cement contractor check it out. You may be surprised at the amount of time, effort, and money it will take to fix.

Structure

Structural problems can be anything from sagging ceilings to creaking floors. However, you can usually tell when there's a serious problem. It shows in the form of cracks everywhere.

If you see a home where there are diagonal cracks at the corners of rooms or, worse, horizontal or vertical cracks running up and down or across walls, assume the worst. Have a structural engineer look at the property.

The same holds true when doors and windows won't easily open and close, when there are cracks in tile on the floor, and when the fixtures in the bathroom and kitchen seem to be coming away from the walls. By themselves none of these may appear to be a serious problem. However, the underlying structure may not be up to snuff and could be the cause.

Correcting structural problems can be as simple as adding a supporting beam under a house or cutting out an entire wall, floor, or ceiling and replacing it. You can hope for the best, but you don't want to get caught with the worst.

TIP

Most structural problems are caused by shoddy construction. The structure may not have been built right. Or substandard building materials may have been used. Or, as in the case where a cement contractor leaves out rebars or wire mesh used to hold the cement together, there may have been cheating going on in the construction phase. That's why any major cracks should be a concern with regard to the structure and the foundation, and you should get professional guidance in judging their seriousness.

Soil

The biggest problem here is usually drainage. If water accumulates around the foundation, it can weaken and eventually destroy it. It can also result in standing water under the home, which can result in mildew and rotted timbers.

Look for high watermarks on the foundation or walls of the basement and under the house. Look for cracked soil under the house that suggests water is there during the rainy season (but may be absent during dry weather).

Call a soils engineer to determine what's causing the problem. It could be as simple as gutter drains aimed toward the house instead of away. It could be as serious as a natural spring under or near the house pushing water up.

Solutions usually involve leading the water out to the front by means of various types of drains. Sometimes a sump pump may be necessary.

TRAP

I once saw a "bargain" house where the entire foundation had been eaten away by a creek that ran under the home. During the dry season, there was no water there. But when it rained, the creek came back and flowed strongly under the house. Unfortunately for the seller, there was no solution that anyone could come up with. Eventually, the house was condemned, bulldozed, and replaced by a tiny park. Some problems have no answer.

Black Mold

This has only recently become a major problem, particularly in states such as Florida and Texas, although it seems to be spreading everywhere. It's not clear whether the problem was always around but unnoticed or just appeared.

Black mold is a hardy fungus that gets into just about everything once it's been established. It can rot wood, drywall, carpeting, furniture—almost anything. And often, it's been around for years before it's discovered.

The real problem is trying to get rid of it. Usually, all the infected areas must be removed and new material put in. Depending on the extent of the infestation, remedying it can be quite costly.

TRAP

Today, many buyers (those to whom you will eventually need to sell) are putting clauses into their purchase contracts about black mold removal. They want sellers to warranty their property against the fungus. The easiest way for you to do this is to inspect the property you're buying thoroughly to be sure it doesn't have any black mold.

Should I Get Permits for the Work?

Put simply, the answer is yes.

I remember an old buddy of mine who used to do a lot of bargain hunting for property. He would buy homes in run-down shape for little money, fix them up, and then resell at a healthy profit. He said he never got a building permit for any of the work he did. His philosophy was, "I'll do the work up to code, but I'm not going to bother or pay for a permit. If they catch me, then I'll simply show them it's good work."

For a while he was okay. Then a property he sold had a small fire, and it was traced back to some rewiring he had done. Because it had never been "permitted," he was suddenly culpable not only for all the repair work after the fire but potentially for criminal charges as well. (Fortunately, no one was hurt, and it was settled amicably.)

However, this story illustrates one of the problems with not getting permits: liability. If you touch the wiring, plumbing, gas, structure, or other systems of the home and there's a problem later on, even if you did a good job, without a permit and approval from a city or county building department, you could be held liable. (You could be held liable even with a permit, but that's a different story.)

As for getting the permit only after you're caught, that makes no sense at all. As anyone who's ever had a permit will tell you, there are two phases to construction. The first is rough, when the work is just patched in; for example, the wires are strung to the outlet boxes. The second is the final, after everything is covered up and painted. The trouble is, if you don't have the rough inspection, you can't really have the final. And once everything is finished, it's too late to have the rough without tearing out all of the finished work. Therefore, getting a permit after the fact usually doesn't work out well.

Permit prices are based on the amount of work done. For small jobs the cost is small. For major renovations they could be expensive. However, you have to build the cost into the price of the property.

I recently put a gas-burning fireplace (a high-tech sealed unit) into a bargain home. Nothing will give me greater pleasure and comfort when I sell than to give the buyer a copy of the building permit showing that everything was done up to code.

What Should I Check for in the Title?

Title problems are usually of little concern in the general home selling market. However, they can be a major concern in the bargain market.

When you buy a house in the conventional way, there is typically an escrow and title insurance. The title insurance company searches the title history of the property and, assuming it's clear, sells you a policy of title insurance for the cost of the home. This is as about as good a guarantee of clear title as you can get.

When you buy an REO property from the bank or some government agency, something similar usually takes place. Although there may or may not be a title insurance company per se involved, the seller or some other company will typically guarantee that:

- The seller does in fact own the property and has the ability to convey it to you.

- (Sometimes) there are no hidden liens or encumbrances clouding the title. This means that there are no unpaid mortgages, tax liens, or whatever.

- (Sometimes) if something should develop impinging on your title, you have somewhere to go to get compensated for the problem.

However, when you buy from a seller who's in foreclosure, or especially, when you buy at a foreclosure sale, tax auction, or similar proceeding, there may be no title insurance and no guarantee that there are no hidden liens against the property. If you're not sure about this, reread Chapters 3 and 11.

How Do I Check the Title?

As noted earlier, you can go to a title insurance company and ask for a preliminary report (prelim) on a piece of property. If you are a frequent customer of the title company, they will typically do this for free. If not, they may charge a few hundred dollars.

The prelim examines the title history and usually reveals any of the problems we've discussed and many others. I've known many investors who get a prelim and if it's clear, go forward with their bid. Many times they are successful, and no problems ensue.

However, a prelim is not title insurance. It does not guarantee against title problems.

But, you may reasonably ask, if the title company has already investigated the property and found nothing, where would title problems come from?

The answer, quite simply, is that the seller, the IRS, a court, or anyone else might slap a lien on the property between the time the prelim was issued and the actual sale. This in fact is more commonly done than most people realize. That's why title insurance companies typically record a title first thing in the morning. They recheck the title the last thing at night to be sure nothing has been slapped onto the title. Then they record the new title (to you) first thing before any liens can be put on. It may sound like tedious work, but the order of recordation is so important that this rigorous procedure is followed.

Thus, if you're a savvy investor, even at an auction you'll endeavor to get title insurance. Some title companies do have ways of issuing a title policy on auction property. You simply have to call and ask.

Barring that, you may want to physically check the title yourself just before the bidding closes and your bid is put in (a sometimes daunting task). This is another reason some investors don't put in their bids until the very last moment.

Thus, when you're dealing with bargain properties, inspecting the title is not so much an option as a necessity.

16

How to Finance a Bargain Property

As an investor, don't expect lenders to welcome you with open arms when you go to finance bargain properties. In fact most lenders will tend to shy away. They prefer owner-occupants.

That's not to say that loans for investors are not available. Today, they are. Mortgages on one- to four-unit properties are available for only a slightly higher interest charge to investors. The only problem is that you'll probably have to put 10 percent down (as opposed to almost nothing down for an owner-occupant).

Can I Get an Owner-Occupant Mortgage?

As noted, this is the very best financing. Whether you're buying independently from someone in foreclosure or an HUD repo, if you intend to live in the property, you'll get first crack at it along with some amazing (close to zero down and reduced closing cost) financing.

Often, the government or other agency will carry the financing itself. For independently owned properties in foreclosure, owner-occupants with a good credit history and adequate income can find loans for as high as 103 percent loan to value (LTV) (check with Freddie Mac). If you are prepared to live in the property, the very best financing in the world is available to you.

So, you may be thinking in a corner of your mind, I'll just say I'm going to live there.

Nope, that's not good enough. We're not talking about pretending to be an owner-occupant. We're talking about actually moving into the home and living there—occupying it.

The great temptation for investors is to say they will live in the property to get the good financing and then not actually move in. By doing so they take advantage of better financing than they could get as an investor. The reason for not moving in, of course, is that they may already have a house in which they live, and they don't want to lose even a month's worth of rent from the property they are buying.

No matter what you call this, it's simple lying, and if you do it, it could land you in real hot water. Lenders are on the alert for people who say they are moving in when they really intend to rent out the property. To confirm that you've moved in, a lender may call after a month or two to check. Or they may send your payment books to your attention at the new home's address with "no forwarding" requested. Or they may even send someone by 3 months later to see how you're doing. If a tenant answers the door, the ruse is up.

And remember, the seller may be an agency of the federal government. Do you want the feds on your case?

Further, almost all mortgages are in some way insured, guaranteed, or resold through government or quasi-government agencies. This means if you lied and are caught, you will have to do a lot of explaining to the Treasury Department. Penalties could be anything from a demand to immediately repay the full amount of the loan to indictment on criminal charges.

Therefore, don't say you're going to live in the property unless you intend to do so. However, having said that, why not consider living in it?

Many investors build up a huge inventory of properties by buying one, moving in, fixing it up, living there for a year or so, and then doing it again with another property. They then rent out the previous home. Why not do this?

There are many considerations. Your spouse may object. Your children may not like transferring to different schools every year. You may not like the neighborhoods in which the bargain homes are located.

Nevertheless, if you're willing to make the sacrifices and move in, you can get a great many bargain homes for next to nothing down.

TIP

Some REO sellers demand that you be a "first-time buyer." Interestingly, this does not really mean it is the first home that you've ever bought. Rather, it means that you haven't bought or owned a home for the previous 3 years. Perhaps it should be called "first time in 3 years buyer."

How Do I Get an Investor Mortgage?

Okay, I haven't convinced you to move in. Then, how do you go about getting a mortgage to buy a property you intend not to move into?

Investor mortgages are generally available for 90 percent loan to value. They are often about an eighth to a half point higher in interest than owner-occupant loans, and they may have an extra point to pay. Additionally, there's a little trick that lenders use for investors who already have rental property that results in their needing higher income to qualify.

If you already own other rental property (as many readers may), the lenders will not allow you to apply all of the rental income you receive toward the new financing. On the other hand, they will require you to note all of the expenses you have. (Recently, they were allowing only about 75 percent of income.) This means that even if your property breaks even, you still need some extra income to balance out the expenses. That's why an investor with multiple properties needs a higher income for the same mortgage than an owner-occupant.

TRAP

Timing is the great key to success in financing bargain properties. If you are buying an REO, you may have only 30 days in which to secure financing. This means you should be preapproved by a lender with only the property awaiting appraisal. If you're buying at auction and need cash, you should obtain a letter of credit from a lender well in advance of the auction. Remember, in many cases if you cannot come up with the cash to pay the REO or the auction seller, you could lose your deposit.

You get an investor mortgage in the same place as you get an owner-occupant loan: a mortgage broker or bank. You simply state what you want the loan for, and the broker or bank will do all the paperwork.

In addition you can also ask the REO seller to carry the financing for you. With 10 percent down (sometimes less), HUD and other agencies will consider carrying the mortgage themselves. If they do, there's usually less paperwork and lower closing costs.

TIP

Above all, learn how much time you have to secure financing and, before making your bid, be sure that you can comply. You don't want to lose your deposit.

What If I Want to Get Cash Out of My Property Later?

Our immediate problem is getting you in. However, once in, how do you get your money back out to reinvest, short of selling? In other words, if you want to keep the property as an investment, how do you cash out?

In the past this was the single most difficult problem for investors. You might buy a bargain and turn it into a solid rental property that produces positive cashflow. Yet, when you wanted to cash out some of your equity, lenders would turn their backs on you.

Today, it's a different story. In most cases you can get an 80 percent mortgage including cash back to you. In some cases 90 percent is available with cash back on a refinance (refi). But you do have to search around.

Again, you'll pay a stiffer interest rate, more points, and need more income to qualify. But at least the financing is usually there.

An alternative is second mortgages. Many banks offer these to investors. Generally speaking, the combined loan to value (CLTV) is the same as for a large first mortgage—80 to 90 percent. However, the higher interest rate and points are only on the second. When this is paired with a lower interest rate first, the combined interest rate can be lower than for a single large new refi mortgage. It's something to consider.

TRAP

You can always go to private lenders who will loan money on secondary financing. However, they tend to charge much higher interest rates, and the loans tend to be for a much shorter term. Go to these lenders when institutional lenders won't touch you.

Are There Any Other Types of Financing?

The first rule in real estate is that everything is negotiable, and the second rule is that creativity pays. There are all sorts of other financing available.

For example, I've seen family financing. A son or daughter may want to buy an investment house. They have the income to handle it but not the cash. So the parents pop for the down payment and closing costs. Then they share ownership. Typically, the son or daughter will handle property management, and when it's time to sell, the profits will be split.

This system is not limited to families. It will work with friends, buddies, or even perfect strangers. However, a word of caution: Put it in writing.

People, even friends and close relatives, often forget what was said months or years earlier. When it's time to sell, you want to have in writing exactly how the profits (or if something goes wrong, the losses) are split. Further, you want to be sure that there are solid escape clauses allowing you, or another party, to exit the deal if situations change. (For example, you could lose your job, or your sibling, friend, son, or daughter could need to move out of the area.)

Therefore, if you intend doing any type of shared financing, spend the bucks to have a good attorney draw up a rock solid agreement. It won't cost that much, and it could save lots of hassle and money later.

TIP

The tax advantages of property ownership (deduction of taxes, interest, and other expenses on investment property) can be divided up in many different ways among shared owners. If this is of interest to you, check in advance with your accountant or tax attorney.

Can I Do Asset-Based Financing?

Yet another type of financing is to borrow on other property, not on the property you are buying. The easiest way to conceive of this is to borrow on stocks or bonds that you own. Very low interest rate loans are available, often through stockbrokers and banks. You can then use this money to purchase new property.

Another method frequently used by experienced real estate investors is to borrow on property they already own to make a new purchase. For example, you may have three rental homes in which you have substantial equity. You now refinance these (either with individual loans or with a blanket loan on all three) and use the funds to buy a fourth house. If you've ever played the game Monopoly®, you know the basics of how this works.

Shoestring Financing

There are other methods of financing that you can try when you really have a bargain and don't have any cash. We'll look into them in Chapter 19.

17

Hidden Treasures in Financing

There's an old saw about real estate that goes something like this. Two fellows are considering the purchase of a skyscraper in Manhattan. The first one says, "The deal's in the bag. We can buy the building for only $100 million."

The second one says, "Sounds terrific. Let's do it."

The first replies, "There's one snag, though. They want $500 in cash!"

In real estate, financing has always been the key. As we've noted earlier, it may not be the price or the condition or the location of the property that makes the deal—it can be the terms.

In recent years, however, it has become fashionable to think of financing strictly in relationship to leveraging. Bargain terms, or bargain financing, has come to mean buying for little or no down payment (see Chapter 19 for suggestions on getting started on a shoestring), but that's not what we're talking about here. In today's market overleveraging and buying with no down payment can be an invitation to disaster.

Finding a bargain in financing rarely means looking for the minimum down payment. Rather, there are other areas that are of strategic importance, such as the specific clauses in the mortgage, its interest rate, and its type.

A Basic Financing Bargain

A friend was recently buying a lakefront lot for investment purposes. The going price for lakefront lots in the area was $110,000. My friend had just closed another deal and had a fair amount of cash. Since he was looking for a bargain, he offered the owner of one of the lakefronts $80,000 cash for the lot.

That was $30,000 less than the market price. Normally, he wouldn't expect an owner to take such a drastic reduction, but cash usually talks. He had hopes of picking up a price bargain by paying for it outright.

The lot owner, however, countered at $105,000. The owner wasn't impressed by cash. (It turned out that she was retired and was befuddled with how she would invest so much cash if she had it.)

My bargain hunting friend was faced with a dilemma. He had hoped to get a price bargain because of his cash offer. Now he discovered that cash wasn't all it was cracked up to be with this owner. So now he did a 180-degree turn and decided to try for a financing bargain. He gave her what she demanded, the full price, $105,000. However, he dictated the terms.

He offered to put 20 percent down. The owner would carry the balance in the form of a mortgage for 15 years at 4 percent interest.

The reason my friend felt this was a bargain was twofold. First, the market interest rate was then 7 percent. (He offered 4 percent.) Second, it's almost impossible to get a mortgage on bare land. If he got the deal, the owner would be financing 80 percent of the purchase price on bare land, a real bargain in itself.

The owner's only quibble was the interest rate. She insisted on 5 percent. But that was still 2 percent below market. And she was willing to give a 15-year loan on a property that no one else would lend money on.

When the price bargain didn't pan out, this bargain hunter sought out and got a financing bargain. (Note that the price was no longer the issue because the terms were so good.)

Understanding Paper

A better-than-market interest rate or a loan that would be otherwise unavailable are two ways to get financing bargains. There are many others. Almost all of these involve the use of paper.

As those familiar with real estate know, *paper* is a term used to describe a mortgage, typically a mortgage taken back by a seller. When you get a mortgage, you've created paper. If someone says she bought a house for $100,000 with $20,000 down and the seller carried the balance, this means that she came up with $20,000 in cash and that the rest ($80,000) was paper.

Here it's important for us to understand a further division. There is *hard* paper and *soft* paper.

Hard Paper

Sometimes also called a *hard-money mortgage,* this is an exchange of cash for a mortgage. You want to refinance your home to take a cruise to Alaska. You go to a lender who gives you $10,000 in cash, in exchange for which you give the lender a mortgage. Because there was cash advanced, this is hard paper. A new first mortgage obtained from a lender to make a purchase of property would be hard paper.

There is no definitive reason why the term *hard paper* is used except that perhaps this is the hard way to finance.

Soft Paper

Also simply called *paper,* this is a mortgage for something other than cash. Almost always it's for equity. A seller wants to get rid of his home. He accepts an offer that calls for him to carry back a second mortgage for $20,000. That amount of money is not advanced in the form of cash to anyone. Rather, it's an equity exchanged for a mortgage. A typical soft-paper transaction might look like this:

Sales price of house	$100,000
Down payment	$10,000
First mortgage assumed by buyer	$70,000
Second mortgage carried by seller (soft paper)	$20,000

Note that in this example the buyer got the benefit of a $20,000 second mortgage without any cash changing hands. Rather, it was the seller who exchanged his equity for the mortgage.

Differences between Hard and Soft Paper

There are two major differences between hard and soft paper. Hard paper almost always carries a higher interest rate. The reason is that when people advance cash, they want to be sure they are earning an interest rate commensurate with the risk.

Soft paper is more flexible. A seller who is taking back a soft-paper second, for example, might just as easily agree to the value of the second being $8000 instead of $10,000 on the purchase of a house. After all, it's the equity that is being exchanged, and it's a lot easier to give up a little equity than to give up cash out of pocket.

Because soft paper is also on equity, not cash, the interest rate might be lower, the terms longer, and the conditions of the loan more favorable. (If we wanted to be precise—as is the case with very large real estate transactions—the exact present value of every mortgage can be calculated from its terms, and we could then accurately compare different mortgages. This, however, is a complex process and beyond the scope of this chapter. For our purposes we need only be concerned with the fact that soft paper is far more flexible than hard.)

Therefore, lenders of hard paper (hard-money mortgages), such as banks, are less likely to offer bargain terms than are lenders of soft paper, such as sellers.

Using Soft Paper to Get Bargains

Some of the best financing bargains come about through the use of soft paper. Once you as a bargain hunter have determined that you are going for a financing bargain (as opposed to a price bargain), there's almost no limit to the creative kinds of mortgages you can develop. It all comes down to negotiation. In most cases this means giving the seller his or her price and getting the terms to suit you.

Each of the following financing bargains assumes that you as a buyer demand particular terms as a condition of purchase. In other words, if the seller doesn't give you the terms you demand, you won't buy.

Getting a Lower Interest Rate

The most obvious kind of financing bargain is to go for a lower interest rate. A seller carrying back paper and getting full price isn't as likely to quibble about interest rates. Such a seller might be happy to accept 5 percent (when the going rate is 7 percent) just to sell the property at full price.

In the negotiations the key is to make the condition of sale the interest rate. Yes, you will pay the price, but only if the seller accepts the rate you demand.

(Note: Accepting a lower than market interest rate can be a problem for the seller. Sometimes the government may "impute" interest in such cases. This means that sellers might have to pay taxes as if they had received market rate, even though they received less.)

Getting a Longer Term

Another bargain area that many hunters overlook is the term. This is particularly the case with bare lots. Most lots are financed by sellers for 3 to 5 years. On the other hand, if you could make a purchase in which the seller agreed to carry the paper for 15 years or longer, it might be a real bargain.

Look at it this way: $30,000 over 3 years at 10 percent interest means that you're going to pay $968 a month, or $11,616 a year. On the other hand, $30,000 over 15 years at 10 percent means that you'll pay only $322 a month, or $3864 a year. It could mean the difference between making a profit or taking a loss.

Negative Amortization

Another use of soft paper is to negotiate for lower payments. The seller is carrying back a $50,000 mortgage at 10 percent interest for 15 years. To fully amortize (pay off) the mortgage, the payments should be $537 per month.

But you plan on renting out the property, and you can't afford to pay more than $450 a month. So you write the mortgage in such a way that your payments equal only $450.

No, that doesn't mean you ultimately pay less. You actually pay more; because you are not paying the full interest due each month, it is added to the mortgage amount (negative amortization), and ultimately you end up owing more than you borrowed. In the meantime, however, you have the advantage of lower payments, which may mean that you can afford to buy a property that you otherwise couldn't afford. (In this case you'd probably figure on refinancing within 5 years to get to a fully amortized, or paid-out, mortgage.)

Deferring the Payments

Yet another financing bargain can be the deferral of payments. You buy a house, and the seller carries back a $20,000 second mortgage at 10 percent. You insist that the terms of the mortgage are no payments at all until it comes due in 3 years.

For 3 years you can thus have the cashflow from the property (from rental income) without making any payments on the second. In times when prices are rapidly rising, this can be a real bargain. It can allow you to buy property with reduced payments, often meaning no negative cashflow. Of course, at the end of the loan term (3 years in this case), it all comes due, meaning that prices had better have risen so that you can sell or refinance.

Some unscrupulous buyers purchase under these terms and then, if prices don't rise, just walk: They drop the property to foreclosure. A foreclosure against a person's record can make it very difficult to get new mortgages in the future. Even if the foreclosure doesn't go against one's record, a reputation as a "walker" will make it difficult for one to deal with buyers in the future.

Paying No Interest

Sometimes sellers are so hung up on price that they are willing to give the buyer interest-free loans. Don't overlook this possibility, rare though it may be. (One of the problems is that the government tends to impute interest, as indicated earlier. This means that sellers may have to pay taxes on interest they did not receive.)

Getting Special Terms

In addition bargains can be found in the terms of the mortgage. These include getting a mortgage that offers:

1. No prepayment penalty (so you can pay it off anytime)

2. Assumability (so the next buyer can assume it)

3. No penalty for late payments

4. A subordination clause (to be discussed shortly)

Getting Money Back Out of the Property

Thus far, we've discussed how to get a financing bargain from soft paper at the time you purchase. Another kind of financing bargain involves getting money out of the property. It is usually done once you have ownership, but in some cases it can be done at the time of purchase.

Simple Refinancing

This is the easiest to understand. You buy a property. It goes up in value. You refinance, getting hard paper (cash for a mortgage), and thus get your money out of your property.

Another way of doing this is to buy distressed property and then fix it up, get it reappraised at a higher value, and refinance it. In this way you can get your cash out without having to wait for appreciation.

Yet another way is to buy income property (an apartment building, for example) and increase the rent. Since the property's value depends on the rent amount, an increase in rent means that your property has increased in value, and you can thus secure a higher loan and get your cash out.

Buying Back the Soft Paper

Another method of getting cash out of property involves soft paper. At the time of purchase, the bargain hunter gives the seller a mortgage for equity. Then, 6 months later, the bargain hunter says to the seller, "I can cash you out. I'll give you 60 percent of the value of that mortgage in cash to pay it off."

Depending on the terms of the mortgage (particularly if it was written for a long term at a low interest rate), the seller might agree. The bargain hunter now refinances the whole property, getting enough to pay off the existing first and the soft-paper mortgage at 60 percent of value. In some cases this can even result in cash going back into the pocket of the buyer.

Cranking the Property

Some bargain hunters specialize in *crankables*, a term which means that the financing on the property allows the buyer to "crank" the property for cash—to get cash back out of the property, usually after purchase.

For those new to finance bargain hunting, this may seem a bit complicated, but it really isn't. The best way to understand it is to see how it works.

Tony bought a house for $100,000. He put $10,000 cash down to a

$90,000 first mortgage. As soon as the purchase was completed, he went out and got a hard-paper second for $20,000.

In this simple example, Tony's refinance brought him $20,000—enough to pay back the original $10,000 he put down plus another $10,000 in his pocket. He "cranked" the property for cash.

Tony's Purchase		Tony's Refinance	
Existing first	$90,000	Existing first	$90,000
Down payment	10,000		
		New second	20,000
Purchase price	$100,000	Total financing	$110,000

Such crankables are easily accomplished in a hot market when property values are rising rapidly. In such a market, lenders of hard paper are frequently willing to lend over and above a recent purchase price because of the rapid price appreciation.

The Subordinated Crankable

Another form of the crankable involves a subordinated mortgage. *Subordination* means that a lender agrees to allow a mortgage to remain in a secondary position. We've already touched on this earlier, and I'll explain it in greater detail shortly. First, however, let's see the effect.

For our example we'll take a theoretical case: Jeff bought a small apartment building for $200,000. The financing was simple. He assumed an existing first mortgage for $100,000, and the owner carried back a second mortgage that was subordinated for $100,000.

Now Jeff decided he needed some cash. So he went out and obtained a new first mortgage for $200,000.

Jeff's Old Financing		Jeff's New Financing	
First	$100,000	New first	$200,000
Second	100,000	Second	100,000
Original financing	$200,000	New financing	$300,000

Suddenly, where there was $200,000 in financing on the property, there is now $300,000. The difference of $100,000 was in the form of cash, which Jeff put into his pocket. He cranked the property for $100,000.

There are two important points to understand about how this was done. First, Jeff secured a new hard-paper first mortgage. First mortgages for cash are very easy to obtain, and the interest rates are highly competitive; when people buy a house, they get a new first. Refinancing as was done here is almost as easy. (On the other hand, hard-money seconds are much harder to obtain, and the term is usually shorter and the interest rate higher.)

Second, Jeff was able to secure a new hard-money first because the existing second mortgage remained in position. Because the second contained a subordination clause, it did not advance to first position upon being refinanced.

TRAP

Sellers who subordinate run the risk of having their collateral evaporate.

Advancement of the Secondary Mortgage. You'll recall that the order of a mortgage depends on when it is placed on the property. The first mortgage was placed first, the second was placed second, and so forth.

As soon as any mortgage is paid off, the mortgages behind it immediately advance in position. This is only logical. If you have a property with three mortgages—a first, a second, and a third—what happens when the first is paid off? You end up with a property that has two mortgages: The second becomes the first, and the third becomes the second. The mortgages advance to fill the empty positions unless there is a special clause in the mortgages (a subordination clause) that forces them to remain in their original position.

When Jeff refinanced, he paid off the existing first on the property ($100,000). Normally, the second would now advance and become a first; however, the second contained a subordination clause that forced it to remain in position.

Thus, Jeff was able to refinance and get a brand new first while holding the second off. The new first was for twice the amount of the old first. Jeff pocketed that money.

Problems with Subordination. What should be apparent is that there is great opportunity for abuse in the subordination clause. If the property was worth only $200,000, then by refinancing the first, Jeff effectively reduced the seller's protection in the property to zero.

Remember, the seller originally gave $100,000 in a second mortgage, and Jeff took over an existing $100,000 first. If the property was worth $200,000, it meant that if the seller had to foreclose, there was enough equity to protect his position. On the other hand, after Jeff refinanced, the first was bloated to $200,000—the full value of the property—and the seller's $100,000 second had no protection. It became worthless. (But if the property had a value of $300,000, then presumably there would have been nothing wrong with refinancing the first for $200,000 because the $100,000 second would still be protected.)

Some sellers have granted subordination clauses in the past (particularly to developers of raw land) only to find that once the new big first was obtained, their interest was unprotected. In the event of foreclosure, they lost everything.

In recent years sellers who have fallen into this predicament have on occasion sued buyers for fraud. This is a strong reason to avoid abuse of the subordination clause.

The Bottom Line

Financing bargains abound. They can be in the form of reduced interest rate, increased term, smaller or no payments, or getting cash out of the property. When the price becomes nonnegotiable (or anytime for that matter), look for a financing bargain.

18
Buying Distressed Property

Distressed property means any kind of real estate that has been neglected, abused, or otherwise damaged. It could mean a house that needs paint, carpeting, and other cosmetic repair work (commonly called a fixer-upper), or it could refer to a property that has been flattened by a tornado. The point is that the damage done reduces the price and means a potential bargain.

Most people think of distressed property as "cheap." It can indeed be inexpensive property, but it can also be top of the line. For example, a friend recently bought a house in the Palos Verdes section of Los Angeles. The house had originally been appraised at $2.3 million, but an earthquake had triggered a landslide, which had severely damaged the property. My friend bought it for $830,000. He then spent another $450,000 pumping a special adhesive mixture into the soil to stabilize it and another $150,000 fixing up the house. His total expenses over 6 months were about $1,280,000. He sold for $2.2 million, netting a profit of $650,000 after sales costs. That was an expensive distressed property bargain!

Not All Distressed Property Is a Bargain

Not all properties that are damaged, however, are bargains. I once remember looking at a house that appeared normal in every way from the front. Walking through to the back, however, I found that a steep landslide had erased the backyard and much of the back of the house.

The property was in an area of $180,000 homes, and the owner was willing to sell for only $90,000—half price. I decided, however, that the property wasn't worth 10 cents, let alone the asking price. The reason was that the landslide had made the lot virtually useless. Even if the present structure was torn down, it is doubtful that it would ever make economic sense to build any other structure there. This was a case not of a distressed but of a deceased property.

The Three Elements of a Bargain Distressed Property

For a distressed property to make economic sense for the bargain hunter, it must not only meet the seven criteria discussed in Chapter 24 for any bargain property. It must also meet the following three criteria:

1. Damage that reduces the price

2. Reparability

3. A true profit margin

The first two are fairly obvious. Without damage the price wouldn't be reduced; therefore, in this type of bargain, we are hoping to find damage that ranges from the simplest cosmetic problems (such as lack of paint) to the most severe structural problems. Damage indicates the possibility of a bargain.

The second element is that, whatever the damage, we must have a successful plan for repairing it. This is the key to dealing with distressed properties. Some enterprising bargain hunters make their fortunes by buying property that everyone else is afraid to touch. They succeed because they have a plan for making repairs. A lot of experience and knowledge are necessary here.

The third element is the one that new bargain hunters in the distressed property field most often overlook. Yet it must be considered before any purchase is made.

The True Profit Margin

The true profit margin (TPM) is the profit that we can expect to make. We determine it by first figuring out how much the repairs are going to cost us and then calculating the margin between our purchase price and the actual market value. Let's take a simple example.

Fran found a house that she felt might be a bargain. It was in a terrible state of disrepair. It had been a rental for years, and the tenants had torn it apart. In addition the house was about 25 years old and desperately needed a new driveway and roof. As she walked through the house, Fran carefully made a list of all the things that needed repairing.

She then contacted different tradespeople and got estimates for how much it would cost to have the work done. (After you've worked distressed properties for a while, you'll get to know these costs automatically.) She added up the costs:

Paint	$2,500
Carpeting	3,500
Roof	8,000
Driveway	2,400
Landscaping	600
Total cost of repairs	$17,000

Fran knew that a similar house in tiptop shape would sell for around $180,000. The owner here was asking $160,000 but had indicated that a lower offer might be acceptable.

Fran decided to offer $150,000. If the owner accepted, she would be getting the property for $30,000 below market. She would then fix it up for $17,000, leaving her a profit margin of $13,000. She considered this to be a good bargain.

Was it? Not really. Fran hadn't considered the TPM. To find the TPM, we must subtract the true costs from the market value:

Market value	$180,000
True costs	
Cost of repairs	−17,000
Liquidation (estimated)	−15,000
Price before TPM	$148,000

Thus, to break even on the deal (zero margin), Fran would need to purchase the property for no more than $148,000. To make a profit, she would need to buy for less. In other words buying for $148,000 was simply not cheap enough. Her costs exceeded her margin, and hence, there was no profit; there was a potential loss of $2,000.

Are the Expenses Realistic?

I am frequently asked if expense figures such as I've quoted here are truly realistic when one is dealing with a distressed property. For example, what if Fran did much of the repair work herself and saved half the cost of the repairs? What if she sold the house "by owner" and saved the commission (together $10,000 or more)? Couldn't she turn a profit by doing these things herself?

My answer is that if you're going to be a serious bargain hunter, then no, you can't count on turning a loss into a profit by doing the work yourself. Here's why.

You Must Pay Yourself a Salary

Regardless of who does the work, it costs money for labor. If Fran paints, fixes roofs and driveways, and installs carpeting, the time she spends doing this work is time she can't spend at some other job. In other words Fran has to pay herself a salary, regardless. Maybe she's unemployed, and this is a way of putting herself to work for a month or more. There's nothing wrong with that as long as we don't confuse working for a salary with making a profit on a property.

Safety Calls for Calculating Liquidation Costs

With regard to the commission and other liquidation costs, I know that some people don't worry about it. They just figure that God will provide a buyer when needed. I don't work that way. To be safe, I feel that one must count on selling the property without a loss as soon as it's fixed up. You may need the cash, you may not be able to rent it, you may become ill and need to get out of the business, or any of a hundred other things could happen; therefore, a quick liquidation should be part of everyone's escape plan (see Chapter 2). Quick liquidations mean paying commissions and other costs. Hence, these costs must be factored in.

Now let's look at some examples of successful distressed property bargains.

The High-Class Distressed Property

I mentioned in Chapter 2 that bargain hunters eventually develop a style, a particular kind and location of property that they look for. At the beginning of this chapter, we saw one bargain hunter whose style is top-of-the-line distressed property. Now we'll consider another and look into the reasons she prefers high-priced properties.

Jane prefers properties in the $300,000 to $500,000 price range. One time, driving out to look at such a property she was considering near Los Angeles, I asked why she specialized in such expensive investments.

"Because the TPM is so great," she said. "Suppose I buy a house that's worth $100,000 for half price. Now say that I have to stick a quarter of its value into repairs. I've thus paid $50,000, and added $25,000 in repairs, making my total investment $75,000. If I now sell for $100,000, I clear $25,000, out of which I may pay as much as $10,000 in commission and closing costs. My eventual profit might only be $15,000.

"On the other hand, suppose I buy a house which will have a market value of $400,000 after I fix it up. I buy for half price, stick the same quarter of its value into repairs, and end up with a $300,000 investment. Now I sell for $400,000 and clear $100,000. Even after taking the commission and closing costs out of this $100,000, I've now got a handsome profit, perhaps enough so that I only need to find two such deals a year." I persisted and asked her how she could buy a house with a market value of $400,000 for half price. "I don't," she said. "I buy it for less!"

Turning Severe Damage into Profit

As we proceeded onto the property, Jane explained her secret. The house was on a hillside, as are many of the homes in L.A. Water runoff had eroded the hill under the house. Part of it was still firmly anchored on its hillside lot, but part, where the land had washed away, was hanging exposed over empty air. The foundation had cracked and fallen away, and that area of the home had slanted precariously downward. Needless to say, the property had been condemned by the city.

"Now that's a distressed house," I said.

"Exactly," Jane nodded. She proceeded to tell me what the present owners had told her. At least half the house would need to be demolished. Then the ground would have to be filled in and packed. Finally, a new structure would have to be built.

"Sounds expensive," I commented.

"About $235,000," she said, "if it's done their way. Instead, I plan to sink three prestressed concrete piers into the soil just beyond the side of the house where the ground has washed away. Then I'll use steel on the piers to form a solid wall, put solid beams under the house, jack it up onto this new foundation, fix any small cracks cosmetically, landscape, and it's done—at $50,000 tops."

"But why don't the present owners do that?"

"They haven't thought of it," she said. "And if they did, they'd probably think the idea was too outlandish to consider seriously."

"So what you're saying is that you'll get the current owners to knock $235,000 off the market value because of the repair work they think is necessary. Then you'll come in and do the work for only $50,000, pocketing the difference of $185,000."

Market value	$400,000
Less estimated cost of repairs	235,000
Owners' reduced price	$165,000
Plus actual cost of repairs	50,000
Total cost	$215,000
Difference (market value less cost)	$185,000

She nodded and then went on to explain the keys to making the deal work: "I have to find property where the problem is severe. I have to be willing to be innovative and to take a chance. That's my risk. The owners have to be convinced that they can't get a better price."

The Secret to Buying the Right Property

One final point: I asked Jane how she was able to locate properties like the one we had seen. "The real secret," she said, "is that the property has to be bad enough that a lender won't give the present owner or some other buyer a new loan. If they can't refinance, then they can't get the money to fix it up themselves, and they have to sell."

I asked Jane if that meant she had to have a lot of cash.

"Yes, I work with cash. But I usually give the owner very little cash for the property—just a mortgage for a short term, say a year, for the equity. When I fix up the property and sell, then I pay off the mortgage.

"I need cash, however, to make the repairs. What I've done is put together a little syndicate of investors. They put up the cash in exchange for a share of the profits. That way I raise the entire $50,000 I need for repairs without having to put up a dime of my own money."

I asked if she didn't have to give the investors some of the profit. "Sure," she said, "but these deals are so fat that there's enough to go around and make everyone happy!"

Jane's style was to work with high-priced properties that had big problems. Not everyone, however, likes to work that way.

The Midpriced Distressed Property

Alice's style was to look for bargains in midpriced property. She preferred standard three-bedroom, two-bathroom homes in blue-collar neighborhoods. This usually meant a market value in the $160,000 to $200,000 range in her area.

I went out with Alice to look at one of her "gems in the rough," as she called them. She referred to her properties as her jewelry.

The house was about 25 years old and located on a fairly heavily traveled street. The location was average—no big pluses or minuses.

From the outside the house was obviously in desperate need of repairs. The moment we entered, our noses curled up. The property had been rented out, and the previous tenants had kept dogs locked inside. The animals had urinated and defecated throughout the house. The smell was horrendous.

As we made our way through the rooms, I noted that the carpet was badly soiled and stained. The walls needed painting and in various places had holes knocked through them. Several doors were missing, and the glass was broken out of the back windows. The kitchen stove was torn apart, and pieces of it were lying about the room. The house had two bathrooms, and both toilet bowls were cracked. One sink had been torn from the wall.

"It's hard to imagine why anyone would do this to a house," Alice commented. I nodded. We had both seen similar damage before.

The backyard was overgrown with weeds, but the real problem was revealed when we looked at the roofline. The timbers holding the roof to the house had buckled for some reason. The result was that the roof had lifted off the house by almost 2 inches at the center. It appeared to be severe structural damage. Alice only smiled. "That's what I was hoping for," she said.

Analyzing the Damage

As we drove back, she explained: "If the house were in perfect condition, it would be worth about $190,000. However, in its present condition, I intend to offer the owner $140,000. I think he might accept for three reasons.

"First, I've investigated and found out that the owner's mortgage is only $120,000, so he has enough equity to sell for what I'm offering. Some properties," she added, "are mortgaged for more than they are worth, so the owners can't sell even if they want to.

"Second, the current damage—and particularly the smell—makes the house's appearance so bad that it's unlikely anyone would rent it or that most people would even consider buying it. Thus, the property is a big headache for the owner.

"Third, regardless of how bad it may appear, all of the damage to the property, except for the roof, is cosmetic. I know it, and furthermore so does anyone who's ever worked distressed property. And the owner probably knows it.

"That's why the raised roofline in the back is so important. It indicates severe structural problems. Nine of ten investors wouldn't touch it. Because of that raised roofline, the owner will be forced to take much less in price."

The Repairs

I asked Alice what she intended to do with the property once she got it. "I'll have it painted inside and out," she said, "have new fixtures installed, have the carpets cleaned, and rent it. I've done it before, and I figure that the total cost will be about $10,000. That will still leave me with a $40,000 equity."

"But what about the raised roofline?" I asked. "What do you plan to do about that?"

"Basically nothing. The house is 25 years old. If the roofline has risen 2 inches in that period of time, I'm not worried. The worst it's likely to do is to rise another 2 inches in the next 25 years. While I'm having the house fixed up, I'll have somebody nail a covering board over the exposed area so that water doesn't get in. I'll probably get it done for under $20."

"You're just going to cover it up?"

Alice looked offended. "Certainly not. It would be immoral and illegal, not to mention the problem to the next buyer. I'll point out that I've sealed the area so that moisture can't get in, and I'll explain exactly my reasoning—that it's a problem, but the likelihood of it getting worse isn't that serious. If the roof doesn't leak and it doesn't look bad, who cares?"

The Secret of Her Success

"The real secret in these midpriced properties," Alice said, "is to find some defect that most people, including the owner, agree is horrible. That becomes a price dropper. What's crucial is for me to know that this horrible problem is either readily correctable or something that I can live with indefinitely."

The Lower Priced Distressed Property

Like Alice, most people are looking for the average house in the average location. But some people find bargains at the bottom of the barrel.

Larry was a bargain hunter who searched for properties in what was a lower economic section of town. Most of these houses were older and less expensive.

"My escape plan doesn't include selling," Larry confided as we drove out to look at a house he was considering. "I'm in strictly for the long run. My goal is to buy, fix up, and rent. I already own 12 properties, and within a year I hope to have 20."

Saying that this was admirable, I then asked what advantage he was particularly looking for in a distressed house. By now we had driven up to the subject property. It was on a quiet street of older and smaller homes. Most, but not all, of the surrounding houses were kept up fairly well.

The subject house, however, was in great disrepair. The front yard was all weeds. As we moved through the house, we could see that it needed painting badly. However, it wasn't in as bad shape as Alice's house had been. The kitchen and the single bathroom were generally in sound condition, as was the roof. It could probably have used a new driveway.

The Advantage of Lower Priced Property

"These houses sell for about $70,000," Larry said. "I look at five or six a week. I'll make a lowball offer on this one of about $55,000. I may have to make a dozen such offers, but sooner or later someone accepts.

"Basically, I buy for no down payment. I look for homes where I can assume the existing financing and give the owner a mortgage for his or her equity. The mortgage is for 15 years and is fully amortized. Eventually, it gets paid off.

"The house looks a lot worse than it is. I have a crew of college kids who'll come in and fix the yard, clean up, paint, and even lay carpet. For about $2000 I can have this house in presentable shape so that I can rent it for top dollar for the area."

Larry's Secret: The Price-to-Rent Ratio

"The key to it all for me," said Larry, "is to buy the properties cheaply enough. If I buy cheaply enough, then the money I get for rents will cover all my expenses. I'll have a positive cashflow.

"This works because rents everywhere have been going up over the past 5 years. Higher priced houses, however, are still much too expensive in most cases to rent for your payments. Low-priced houses are different. There, you can frequently rent for more than the payments.

"Take this house, for example. If my offer is accepted, I'll have bought it for $55,000 with no cash out of my pocket. (Of course, I'll spend $2000 fixing it up.) My payments, including everything, will be about $600 a month, yet I can rent it easily for about $700. That puts a positive cashflow of $100 per month into my pocket.

"In addition I start off with $20,000 equity in the property, and that builds. And there are the tax advantages. Finally, I can eventually raise rents and improve my cashflow picture enormously."

The No-Liquidation Escape Plan

I pointed out that if he had to liquidate, he wouldn't have much profit at all.

"Of course, you're right," he said. "But my escape plan only calls for liquidation in an emergency. I buy at least $10,000 below market. If I have to sell, even adding my costs of fixing up, I can get out without being hurt. I won't make a profit, but I won't lose either.

"On the other hand, I'm not buying to sell. I'm buying to keep and hold. Since I buy so low, I can get property that I can rent out and make a positive cashflow on."

Larry's price-to-rent ratio was a minimum of 1 percent. He would only buy a property if he could rent it for at least 1 percent of the purchase price. The higher the ratio, of course, the better. This meant that a property that was worth $70,000 had to be rentable for at least $700 per month. (In this case it was right on the money.)

Commercial Opportunities

Thus far, we have only considered distressed homes. But all kinds of property can fit this category—for example, commercial property.

I recently looked at a piece of commercial real estate that was truly distressed. It was a fairly large lot zoned commercial. In the front of the lot was a closed, broken-down hamburger stand needing repairs. At the back of the lot was a do-it-yourself car wash. In the middle was a garage for the storage of cars. The only part of the property that was currently bringing in income was the storage garage.

I didn't want this property for myself (for reasons I'll discuss shortly). But a friend, George, whose style was commercial property, was thrilled by it.

We estimated the value of the lot to be $75,000. The value of the hamburger stand and car wash could only be estimated on the basis of the net income they could produce. George estimated that in good working condition they would bring in a combined $1000 per month, or $12,000 per year. Using a gross multiplier of 8 as a guesstimate (see the section "Terms Bargain" in Chapter 24 for an explanation of such multipliers), he estimated their worth at about $96,000. The garage was bringing in $300 per month, or $3600 per year, so he guessed its value to be about $29,000.

Lot alone	$75,000
Hamburger stand and car wash	96,000
Garage	29,000
Commercial property value	$125,000

Calculating the Bargain

"I'll offer the owner $85,000," George said. "I've already checked the financing, and that's about what he owes. In other words I'll take it off his hands. Of course, he may counter, but I'm willing to pay up to $90,000 for the property."

"An income property's value is based on the income it produces," he noted. "In this case it's got almost no income. Apparently, the owner isn't able to get it up and running so it can produce income; hence, he must already be expecting to sell for a loss. He has a headache here that I can cure for him."

I asked George how he was figuring the deal.

"Easy," he said. "The hamburger stand probably cost only $20,000 to build brand new. I'll spend $5000 and have it in tiptop shape. Another $2000 will put the car wash back in business. I'll lease both out and collect the rents.

"Once everything is back in operation, I'll have a property worth $125,000 that I bought for at least 25 percent off. I can hold it for rental income or sell it for profit. That's what I call a bargain."

Getting Out of Your Style

I left George blissfully pondering what he would call his new hamburger stand. (He ended up calling it "Gorilla George's Gourmet Burgers.") For him it was indeed a bargain. But it wasn't for me, and it may not have been for you.

The reason has to do with style. My own style with regard to distressed property involves residential real estate. I feel comfortable there. I know I can rent it out, and I know what I need to do to get the property in shape to attract tenants.

On the other hand, I don't know anything about the car wash business or the restaurant business. Yes, I might be able to find a tenant to lease out these businesses. But I really don't know how to fix the property up to attract that tenant. And here (in contrast to my residential properties) I don't know a good tenant from a bad one. My point is that in this case the distressed bargain was only a bargain for the right person whose style involved commercial property. George immediately knew what to do and how to do it. I didn't.

What's more, I had no desire to learn. I like my style and want to stick with it.

Location Bargains

The final distressed property bargains we'll consider are location bargains. This is stretching our definition of a distressed property a bit, but I think it'll be worth it.

Donna liked location bargains. Recently, she took me out to see her latest purchase. We drove to a fancy neighborhood. It had big new houses interspersed with older and much smaller homes.

"This is a jumbled neighborhood," she said. "Big new houses in the $350,000 price range mixed with little old houses selling in the $150,000 price range." We drove up to her new purchase. It was a little old house. "If this house were anywhere else in town, it would probably sell for $120,000. But in this neighborhood I paid $145,000 for it.

"What I'm going to do is to refurbish and add on to it. I'll probably spend $125,000 adding a new master bedroom and renovating the kitchen and baths. When it's finished, the house will look like one of the big houses in this neighborhood. I'll put it up for sale for $350,000 and make $80,000 profit before sales costs."

I mention Donna's style only because quite a few bargain hunters are using it. Looking for jumbled neighborhoods in which the smaller houses are really location bargains can pay off. The technique, however, usually requires a fair amount of cash to pull off.

The Bottom Line

Some people worry that there aren't distressed property bargains out there. They lament that these properties get scooped up as fast as they come on the market.

It isn't necessarily so. Some properties have severe problems and stay on the market for months waiting for the right person with a solution. New ones are coming up for sale constantly.

There are still distressed properties out there and lots of them. You have to look carefully. Also be sure that you really do have the experience and knowledge to pull off the solution you have in mind.

19
Getting Started on a Shoestring

Do you need a lot of cash to be a real estate bargain hunter? No, you don't, but it helps. As seen in other chapters, opportunities do exist for those with little or no cash. (Of course, if you do have some capital, it's a big advantage.)

This chapter is for those who are getting started here and now but don't have very much cash. You want to become a bargain hunter, and you need some capital to get started. How do you raise it?

A special word of warning to readers. Don't gamble with money you can't afford to lose. If your savings or other cash holdings are irreplaceable and you're counting on them for retirement, health security, or other similar reasons, don't risk them on a real estate bargain. There are no sure things in life, and real estate is no exception. You could lose. If you can't afford to lose the money you have, you're probably not the right person to be involved in hunting for bargains. Not everyone is. Only if you have the financial stability to sustain a possible loss and continue on without difficulty should you dabble in investment real estate.

Now, how do you raise the necessary capital? Here are some clues.

Don't Overlook Any Possibilities

How you raise capital to get started in bargain hunting can run the gamut from something simple like cashing in savings bonds to something unusual like putting together a syndicate of your relatives and friends. The important point to remember is that once you've found a bargain property, you don't want to lose it for lack of capital. When you see the opportunity to make thousands of dollars in quick profits, you don't want to be a dollar short of getting in.

Thus, ideas that may sound outlandish right now while sitting comfortably and reading this book may prove to be lifesavers later when you desperately need to raise the dollars to buy the property. My suggestion is that you dismiss no notions out of hand.

Someday you may fall into a terrific bargain opportunity and need only a few more dollars in cash to swing it. You're ready to sell your brother's last pair of pants to get the money. When that time comes, remember this chapter. Come back and reread it. Maybe, just maybe, one of those ideas that before seemed so unlikely may seem a bit more practical . . . and possible.

Raising Money for the Down Payment

When I talk about raising capital, I'm speaking about raising enough money for the down payment. In almost all cases, a large part of the purchase price can be financed. Typically, this down payment will be anywhere between 5 and 20 percent of the total cost. That's the amount you'll need to raise in cash. (The balance will come from a mortgage, either from an institutional lender like a bank or from the seller.)

The question here is how do you get that down payment?

TRAP

There are lots of books written on how to buy property without a down payment; if you follow their advice, you probably can purchase that way. But here we're concerned with getting bargains. Unless you plan to make hundreds of offers in the hope of finding that one seller who will go along with a no-down scheme and still give you a bargain (a tiring and discouraging plan), it's best to figure you'll need some cash down.

How to Get Cash

You have a variety of ways to raise cash. As I mentioned at the outset, don't discard any of them. You never know when one or another of these ways may pull out the money you need to make a deal.

Write a Check

Too simple? Not if you don't have money in the bank. But planning ahead can help even when you don't have the money. Most banks today allow reserve and overdraft privileges for customers who first establish a line of credit. Typically, these credit lines allow the customer to write a check to anyone for amounts up to $100,000 without a cash balance. The bank honors the check and converts the money into a short-term loan.

If you're planning to be a bargain hunter, go down to your bank right now, today, and take out a line of credit on your checking account. Go for the highest limit you can get. It's easiest to establish this credit line before you need the money. (Remember, you must pay this money back, so be sure your overall plan takes this into account.)

Withdraw Your Savings

Strange as it may seem, some bargain hunters plan on doing their investing without touching their savings. Admittedly, bargain hunting is a risky business. But you have to pay the toll to play the game. That may mean depleting your savings account.

TRAP

Don't gamble with money you can't afford to lose.

Cash In Your Stocks, Bonds, Coin Collection, or Other Investments

Most of us try to diversify our investments. But what if a fantastic real estate opportunity appears? Should we turn it down simply on the general principle of diversification? Maybe. On the other hand, if you're really convinced that this is the deal of the century, perhaps you'll want to consider selling stocks, bonds, rare coins, diamonds, gold, or whatever other investments you have. If the opportunity truly is good, maybe you could make more by putting all your eggs in this one basket.

Sell or Refinance Your Property

Do you have any property you can sell? Do you have an investment piece
of real estate? What about a boat, car, motorcycle, or even furniture? It's a
matter of compromise. Are you desperate enough to sell or refinance some
item you now own to get the real estate bargain you've found?

Sell Your House (and Move to an Apartment)

I said some of these suggestions would sound outrageous. But consider
that you've found a terrific bargain. It can make you thousands, perhaps
tens of thousands. You need cash right away, and the only collateral you
have is your house. Assuming you can't borrow on it (which we'll discuss in
a moment), consider selling it. It's an asset, and if you're really desperate,
it can get you cash.

Borrow

Finally, if all else fails, you can borrow the money. We've already talked
about one form of borrowing—writing a check on a line of credit. In addition you have many other opportunities for borrowing.

Borrow on Real Estate

Can you borrow a hard-paper or hard-money second on the property
you're buying or on some other property (such as your home)? In most
cases lenders want a first-mortgage position. But some lenders for very little more interest will make second mortgages. Some will make thirds.
Don't overlook these secondary positions for raising cash.

Borrow from a Bank

Banks will make real estate loans. In addition banks will make loans on
other collateral, such as your car, furniture, or stocks. In some cases, if you
have good credit, they will make unsecured loans—that is, a loan on just

your good name. If you have good credit, a bank is a "must see" source for cash.

Borrow from a Credit Union

If you belong to a credit union, you can frequently get either a secured or an unsecured loan, often at a favorable interest rate. Don't overlook this possibility. A simple call to your credit union should let you know your chances of getting money from this source.

Borrow on Your Credit Cards

If you have reasonably good credit, you should be able to get a VISA card and/or MasterCard. If you can get one such card, you can get dozens. Banks and other institutions compete with one another to offer you these cards. For an annual fee of around $50 per card, there probably isn't any limit to the number you can get. (I once knew an individual who had acquired over 50 such cards. I've heard of people who have acquired hundreds!) Each card usually offers anywhere from $300 to $25,000 in credit. For a short-term loan, you can borrow the limit on each and get a substantial amount of money.

But remember, you'll have to pay it back at a high interest rate, often 20 percent or more, and there could be annual fees. Be sure your plan calls for a way to repay the funds with any interest.

Borrow from Friends

It's hard to ask friends for loans. On the other hand, if it's the only way to raise money for a terrific opportunity, why not try? It sometimes helps assuage any feelings of guilt if you offer to repay with interest. Another consolation can be to take the friends in as partners. We'll discuss this shortly.

Borrow from Relatives

If it was hard to ask friends for loans, think about asking relatives. I consider this close to a last resort approach. Nevertheless, if it's the only way . . .

Borrow from a Commercial Finance Company

I do consider this a last resort. Some of these companies will lend you money at very high interest rates only if they tie up virtually all your assets, including both personal and real estate. And they may not feel any restraint at foreclosing, repossessing, and garnishing wages to collect their due.

Use them only if you must. Even then, borrow as little as possible.

Clues on Borrowing

There are lots of books and magazine articles constantly appearing that give you hints on borrowing, including methods of improving your credit. Check with them. In the meantime here are five clues to borrowing that you may find helpful.

Only Borrow When You Don't Need the Money

Lenders hate loaning to someone in need. They feel that such a person may be desperate enough to exaggerate (if not lie) on loan applications. Therefore, if you really need the money quickly, you may have trouble getting it.

The answer is to arrange for a loan before you need it. Get the credit line or loan established. Then, when you find the deal, the money's waiting.

Establish Your Credit

If you have no credit, go into a bank and open a checking account and a savings account. After a month or two, apply for a credit card. Your bank will probably give it to you, although at a low limit. Charge up to the limit and repay on time.

Now go back to the bank and take out a personal loan. (They'll undoubtedly give this to you based on your checking and savings accounts and credit card history.) Repay the loan promptly when due. You should now have enough credit to qualify for other credit cards and loans.

Improve Your Bad Credit

If you can't get a credit card (the one sure sign of bad credit), try buying a house to improve your credit. It's not that hard. Find a seller who will go for nothing or little down (the seller carries a second or third mortgage for the down payment) and who has an existing loan that is fully assumable. (You're not going to get a bargain here. This is only to establish credit.)

Once you buy the house, make all the payments on time. Now reapply for either a bank loan or a credit card. With the house as collateral and with the evidence of prompt payment on the mortgage, you should find it much easier this time around.

Borrow All That You Need the First Time

No lender likes to see the borrower coming back asking for more money. It indicates that the borrower didn't have enough foresight to know how much was needed or miscalculated or is in trouble. You may not get a second chance. Therefore, overestimate your need and borrow the full amount.

Pay Back Promptly

The only thing worse than failure to repay is delayed repayment. A late payment goes on your record every month. (Failure to pay appears only once.) If you value your ability to borrow, always repay everything you borrow promptly.

Sources of Collateral

Lenders want collateral. They want to get something substantial if you fail to repay what you borrow. (In some cases, if you have very good credit, a lender will give you an unsecured loan. If that's your situation, you needn't worry here. Sometimes you can also get unsecured loans from friends and relatives.) Here are some ideas on what you can put up as collateral:

1. Your house.

2. Other real estate, including lots, second homes, and investment properties.

3. Personal property, including car, stereo equipment, and furniture.

4. Your life insurance. If you have a policy that has equitable value, you can probably borrow against it at a bank. (Dangerous.)

5. Treasury bills, certificates of deposit, stocks, bonds, second or other mortgages in your favor, or any other financial instrument of value.

6. Your retirement account. (Dangerous.)

7. Your salary. Sometimes, particularly with banks, just being able to prove ability to repay is sufficient. A steady job means a lot, particularly if it goes with good credit. For more money you might want to try a second job.

Note: Don't touch life insurance or retirement income if it's money you can't afford to lose.

Try an Exchange

This idea is overlooked too often. Instead of putting up cash for the down payment, will the seller accept something else? What about offering a lot you own in trade? What about another piece of investment property? What about a car, motorcycle, boat, furniture, or other item you own? If you have a skill (such as being an accountant or carpenter), can you exchange your future work for the down payment?

You'll never know what the seller will trade for until you ask.

Take In a Partner

In my opinion this should be a very last resort. I know that many real estate agents and investors advise the partnership approach to raising capital. In my own experience, however, I've found that taking in a partner means adding a headache.

Invariably, your ideas and expectations are going to differ from your partner's, and this can lead to hurt feelings, tension, or even lawsuits. It can all be avoided by not having partners.

On the other hand, having now stated my own preference, if you are still determined to move ahead with a partnership, there are two types that have been very popular.

Syndication

Syndication is a term commonly used in real estate to describe a "limited partnership." In a typical limited partnership, you put up your expertise and others put up the money. The idea is that if you want to raise $30,000, it's a lot easier to find 10 people willing to put up $3000 apiece than to find one willing to risk the entire $30,000. Syndication is a way of bringing partners into a real estate deal.

In a limited-partnership syndication, there are typically two different types of partner. There is the general partner (you) who is responsible for everything that happens (including foreclosure and personal injury lawsuits). Then there is the limited partner who invests the money and hopes to get part of the profit but who has very limited exposure and liability. For friends and relatives who want to invest, this can be an excellent capital-raising device.

It must be understood, however, that a limited-partnership syndication is a legal device. It is regulated by the state you are in and in some cases by the Securities and Exchange Commission. Unless you have had great experience with it, you should not attempt to create it yourself. Rather, it's something that requires the services of an attorney to set up.

Equity Sharing

This is a method of splitting up the parts of an investment between the needs of two (or more) people. Typically, one person finds the deal and handles the cashflow (collects rents and makes payments), and the other person has the cash but doesn't want to bother getting his or her hands dirty playing around with the property.

The two buy a bargain property together, one contributing cash, the other expertise, and they later split the profits. Sometimes it works out quite well.

The essence of equity sharing is the agreement between the partners. It must specify who is to put up what and how the profits are to be divided later. It should also set down the procedure for handling any unforeseen problems that might arise.

Unfortunately, most attorneys don't have the opportunity to work with many equity-sharing agreements. Thus, randomly walking into an attorney's office and asking him or her to create an equity-sharing agreement could be costly and may produce spotty results.

This agreement requires an attorney who specializes in real estate and who handles equity-sharing agreements on a regular basis. Such an attorney can whip one together to fit your needs in a very short time and, ideally, at a very reduced cost.

The Bottom Line

These, then, are some of your options when you need to raise cash. The important point to remember is that if you need to raise cash for a terrific deal, then in most cases you'll find the money. If the deal is really good, you may have to tell someone else about it (such as a friend or relative), but one way or another, you'll come up with the dough. People like you won't let a terrific opportunity for profit slip through their fingers without a good fight. It's better, of course, if you're prepared in advance and don't have to give away the gravy in the transaction just to be able to put it together.

20
Bargains in the MLS and FSBOs

There are two acronyms that every bargain hunter should know: MLS (multiple-listing service) and FSBO (for sale by owner). I'm sure some investors are critical of finding bargain properties through agents' and owners' listings. Perhaps you've heard the comments? "If there were any good listings out there, agents would have bought 'em themselves." And, "By-owner sellers always ask too much for their properties."

There's certainly truth in both perspectives. If there's a bargain that comes up on the MLS, agents will sometimes buy the property for themselves. And as a general rule, FSBOs do tend to ask too much for their property.

But it's not always that way. I've seen amazing bargains crop up on the MLS and just sit there, waiting for someone to take advantage of them. And sometimes FSBO sellers do offer their properties at bargain prices. If your mind is closed to these opportunities, you'll never find them. But it's important to be willing to check out *all* possible sources of bargain properties.

Can I Find Bargains on the MLS?

Of course, many are there. First, let's dispel the notion that agents always buy up MLS bargains.

I've been an agent and know a lot of agents, and I can tell you that by far, agents would rather make a commission than buy a property. Remember, real estate is their bread and butter. If they don't get those commissions, they don't have an income. And almost always, income is more important (certainly more immediate) than long-term investment. Therefore, many an agent will gladly pass a bargain on to you and collect the commission.

This doesn't mean, however, that you have all the time in the world to act. On a typical MLS there will be hundreds, perhaps thousands, of houses. However, there are likewise going to be hundreds and thousands of buyers looking at these. Some are plain old homeowners looking for a new residence. But others are investors. And you have to be quick on your feet to beat them out.

That's why I suggest you make good friends with an agent, preferably a Realtor® (a member of the National Association of Realtors) and someone who is on the local MLS. Tell this agent exactly what type of property you're interested in. Let him or her know how much you have to invest and how quickly you can move once you find the right property.

If you've got a good agent, he or she will always keep you in mind. Many times agents hear of bargains even before they hit the MLS, and your agent can quickly call you. You can check out the property, make your offer, and ideally, get the good deal. However, none of this will happen if you don't have a Realtor looking out for you.

Should I Check the Old Listings?

Yes, certainly. Especially look for those that have been listed a long time. You might find a seller who's very anxious to sell and may be willing to accept a lowball offer. Any seller who's had a property on the market for 3 to 6 months with no activity is likely to be very anxious to make a deal and cut the price to do it. In other words look for the "stale" listings, those that have been out there the longest.

Also look for big price reductions. A seller who sees his or her property sitting there and not drawing buyers may decide to spur activity by dropping the price. This often happens, and small reductions are common. It's the big price reduction that indicates a seller who wants to move a property quickly and is trying to draw attention to this fact.

Multiple price reductions indicate a very anxious seller, particularly when they come close together. I once bought a home from sellers who were so anxious to sell that they were cutting their price $10,000 a week until the property was sold. If I had waited long enough, I might have gotten the property for almost nothing, although someone else would have bought it long before then.

Also keep in mind that when you find a property that has been reduced in price, don't feel you have to offer the current asking price. A price reduction is just a "come-on." For you it means it's time to submit a lowball offer.

No, you won't have them all accepted. You may not have most accepted. But if every once in a while you do get one accepted, you will have found a good bargain.

Should I Bother with the Legwork?

Learn to farm. No, this doesn't mean study for an agricultural degree. It does mean that you learn to know several nearby neighborhoods very well. This is helpful whether you're looking for foreclosures, REOs, MLS, or FSBO properties.

Farming means picking an area and, like a farm, cultivating it. Drive the streets and look for signs. You may have gone right past a written description in the MLS book and a listing's picture because they didn't seem to offer much. But when driving by the house, you immediately see that it's distressed or has some other feature that suggests it's a bargain. Maybe you'll find this wonderful property because you take the time to check it out while other investors sit at home waiting for bargains to come to them.

TIP

Some of the most successful real estate investors are property "farmers." They select several neighborhoods or parts of town and farm the area. They scrutinize every property that's for sale, and when something good turns up, they're the first to know about it and recognize it for what it is.

Are There Bargains in FSBOs?

Certainly, but they're not common. Most FSBOs tend to want more for their property than the market bears. Indeed, one of the more common reasons that people sell on their own is because they think their property is worth more than real estate agents tell them they can get for it. It's a kind of mentality that says, "I'll show you what my house is really worth!"

In addition most also want to save on the commission. On a home in the $300,000 price range, a typical 6 percent commission is $18,000. That's a lot of money, and it's a big incentive to want to sell it yourself and save.

Thus, most FSBOs are going to be a waste of your time. But not all.

Occasionally, you'll come across the FSBO seller who is more realistic. This person has thought it through. If the house next door is listed and is selling for $300,000, at a 6 percent commission the seller is only getting $282,000. If the FSBO places it for sale at $282,000, he or she will get the same net amount. However, the property will be 6 percent less in price than a comparable property. It's a bargain that will more likely attract buyers, including you.

Further, if the seller is highly motivated to sell (see Chapter 21), he or she may drop the price even further. These sellers want action now. And lowering the price is the way to get it.

This is not to say that you should pay the asking price, low as it might be. You will still want to negotiate and make a lowball to see how motivated this seller really is. Depending on your negotiating skills and the FSBO's motivation, you could find a true bargain here.

TRAP

 Buying FSBO is almost always more difficult. You don't have an agent to handle the paperwork and the negotiations. You have to do it face-to-face, and for many people this is difficult in the extreme. On the other hand, if it's something with which you really don't feel comfortable, you can always hire your own real estate agent. Today, many agents throughout the country will work on a fee-for-service basis. On the East Coast, many real estate attorneys will do the same thing. Find a good FSBO, but don't want to do the dirty work? Hire a professional to handle it for you. For more information on fee-for-service professionals, check my book *Getting Started Investing in Real Estate* (McGraw-Hill, 2002).

21
Buying from Motivated Sellers

"One man's wine is another man's poison," or so goes the old saw. So it can also be in real estate. What can be a horrible property to one person can be a treasure to another.

For one reason or another, some sellers are "motivated" (a term frequently used by brokers in reference to sellers who are willing to make the concessions necessary to sell a property quickly). They want desperately to get rid of a house, office building, or lot. To accomplish this, they are willing to lower the price, offer enticing terms, or both. On the other side can be the bargain hunter for whom a lower price or better terms (or both) is just what he or she is looking for. Put a motivated seller together with the bargain hunter and you can have a marriage made in heaven.

Who Are Motivated Sellers?

Sellers can be motivated for a wide variety of reasons. Some of the reasons may be personal and have nothing to do with the property. Others can be directly related to the real estate itself. Here are a few of the reasons that a seller may be motivated:

Can't manage the property (can't collect rents)

Payments too high

Just doesn't like the property

Divorce

Job relocation

Lost job and now faces foreclosure

Death in family

There are other motivations, but whatever the actual distress may be, it motivates the seller to act quickly. Hence, we find a bargain.

Ethical Considerations

It's important to understand that when we speak of dealing with motivated sellers, we are not talking about taking advantage of someone. The bargain hunter did not create the problem for the seller and is not contributing to it. Rather, the bargain hunter is offering a solution.

It's easiest to understand this in economic terms. If you're selling something and aren't motivated, you can ask the highest price and offer the least desirable terms. Because you're not motivated to sell, you can sit back and wait months, or perhaps years, until the market catches up with you and a buyer finally thinks that what you're offering is worthwhile.

On the other hand, if you are highly motivated to sell, you can't afford to wait. You want to deal now, immediately, today. Consequently, you must lower your price and offer more desirable terms. You keep on making the property increasingly attractive until you finally induce a buyer to make a quick purchase.

In terms of who's doing whom a favor, the seller is doing the buyer a favor by offering a more attractive deal, and the buyer is doing the seller a favor by purchasing the property fast. It's a mutually beneficial arrangement that makes sound economic sense.

Finding Motivated Sellers

Motivated sellers can be anywhere. Their property may be listed with brokers. It may be offered for sale by the owner (FSBO). It may not yet even be on the market.

Pete was a bargain hunter. He made no secret of the fact. He had gotten to know half a dozen different brokers in his area, and they were all out scouting property for him (see Chapter 22, "Getting Brokers to Work for You").

One day a broker named Juanita called him. She told him of a property she had discovered. It had a motivated seller. Pete listened carefully.

The property was a house in an average area of the city. It had just been listed by another broker, who had put it on the multiple-listing service. It would be a day or two before a written notice of the listing went out to all the brokers who belonged to the MLS. But information on the property was immediately available to any agent who wanted it through the computerized listing service. As soon as a property was listed, it came on the system.

Juanita made it a point to check her computer each morning and found the property there. She had promptly investigated it.

Offering a Bargain for a Quick Sale

The owner wanted a quick sale, that week if possible, and as short an escrow as could be arranged. He had lung cancer, knew he was dying, and wanted to dump the house and move across the country to spend the rest of his days where he grew up. His motivation was that he knew he didn't have a lot of time. He wanted to sell within 1 or 2 days.

His house was a three-bedroom, two-bathroom model. In his area this model normally sold for $105,000 in good condition. His property was in good condition. Moreover, he had added on a new fourth bedroom and a dining room. In addition he had converted the garage to a family room and built a separate detached two-car garage. Finally, he had poured a lot of concrete so that there was room to park a recreational vehicle by the side of the house.

The additions added a minimum of $10,000 to the value of the property, making it at least a $115,000 house. However, to be sure of a quick sale, he was asking what he felt he had in the property—$89,950. The house was at least $25,000 below market.

Juanita suggested that Pete immediately look at the property and make an offer. Pete took his lunch hour to examine the property and then made an offer. He offered full price.

Juanita presented the offer at three o'clock that afternoon. The seller accepted, provided that Pete would release $2500 from escrow to him as soon as he signed off; the seller wanted to leave at once.

Normally, releasing money from escrow is a bad practice; if the deal doesn't close, you could lose your money. However, Pete agreed, provided that a preliminary title report showed the property had no title defects and provided that the seller signed all documents. Three days later Pete released the money and the seller left. Three weeks later the property transfer was formalized.

Pete had used an agent to find a highly motivated buyer to make a quick profit. Although motivated sellers such as this don't crop up every day, they are out there. (You will see in Chapter 22 how to get agents to find them for you.)

Desperately Seeking
a Way Out

Tilly was a bargain hunter looking for motivated owners. Her specialty was apartment buildings. She would drive around the city looking at such buildings. When she found one that looked run-down, she would contact a tenant to find out who the owner was and then call up the owner and ask if he or she would like to sell.

Most owners said that they would indeed like to sell. But they immediately asked a price that was unreasonably high, usually higher than the market value of their property. They weren't motivated to sell; hence, they could ask any price and then sit back and wait.

Eventually, Tilly inquired about an eight-unit building in a less desirable part of the city. She had thought this might be a winner for her because three of the units were vacant and the place was dilapidated (nothing serious, just needed some TLC). The tenant she spoke to laughed at the mention of the landlord, saying that she was 3 months behind in her rent.

The Absentee Landlord

The property owner was a draftsman who worked in a neighboring city. He had traded two rental houses he owned for the apartment building, which had been nothing but a headache ever since. At first he had used a management company to handle the building's rentals. However, the management fee was a thorn in his side. When fully rented, the building brought in $2400 per month, which just equaled the payments. However, the management fee was 15 percent more, or another $360 that he had to take out of his pocket each month. In disgust he had finally fired the management company.

That's when his troubles really started. He didn't have the time or the mental fortitude to go around collecting rents. So he let things slide. Now most of the tenants were months behind. His halfhearted attempts at renting had not worked. He just didn't have time to run out and show the property when a prospective tenant wanted to see it. He had gone from the frying pan into the fire, for in place of paying only a management fee, he was now taking even more money out of his pocket to cover the mortgage payments.

The owner had a headache and desperately wanted to get rid of it. He had a $50,000 equity in the property from the two rental houses he'd traded for it. He said he wanted to save his equity, or as much of it as possible, but he also wanted to get rid of the property in the worst way. It had been interfering with his work. He was sorry he had ever heard about it. He was thinking of listing it that week with a broker.

Tilly told him not to list or else she would not buy. She also said she'd be back with an offer in 24 hours.

Tilly did some homework. The property was worth $200,000, and it had $150,000 in loans against it. The owner wanted out in the worst way.

Tilly's Offer

Tilly offered the owner $165,000. She would assume the existing financing and give him a note for $15,000. She would put out no cash of her own.

The owner was at first flabbergasted and then angry. "You're trying to steal my property!" he exclaimed.

"Not at all," she said. "If you try to sell it, you'll have to knock down the price by at least $10,000 because of the way it shows. It's got vacancies, the tenants you have aren't all paying, and it looks like a mess. I'll have to take money out of my pocket to fix up the place.

"In addition you'd have to pay a commission if you sold it through an agent. Assuming the commission was 6 percent, that's another $12,000. If you add those two amounts together, it comes to $22,000. That's your basic deduction for selling the property, and it lowers your net proceeds from the sale to $178,000.

"Then you'd have to sit on the property for 6 months or longer waiting for it to sell. During that time you'd be losing thousands by making up mortgage payments, taxes, and insurance out of your own pocket. I'm offering you $165,000 to make a deal today. Take my price and you'll be done with your headache immediately."

Market value in top shape	$200,000
Deductions	
Off for present condition	10,000
Normal 6 percent commission	12,000
Premium for a quick sale	13,000
Total	$35,000
Tilly's offer	$165,000

The owner considered only a short time and then took it. Tilly got the property for $35,000 off market value. Of course, she had to do some clean-up work. However, she was an expert at managing, and she had the building filled with paying tenants within a month.

Motivated Sellers Are Out There

Both of the preceding stories are based on true incidents. They are not unusual. Motivated sellers are out there. It may take some creative effort to find them (either with the help of brokers or by looking yourself), but once you do find them, you can be on the trail of a real bargain.

There are at least two sources that can lead you to motivated buyers. In the case of investment property, as we saw in the example with Tilly, the biggest headache is management. Some people, a great many people, simply can't handle management. They don't want the stress of collecting rent and dealing with tenants. Yet because they've heard of all the wonderful profits available in real estate, they've bought investment property. Now they have a bigger financial headache than they ever thought possible. Usually, they are taking money out of their pockets each month just to keep the property solvent. They think of their investment as a running wound that they would do almost anything to get rid of.

For the bargain hunter, therefore, one source is to search for badly managed property. This can be anything from a single-family residence to an office building. Badly managed property stands out. It looks bad. Once you find one, locate the owner. It doesn't hurt to ask if he or she wants to sell, and it could result in a great bargain.

Another source is the seller with a personal problem. As in our first example, the seller may want to sell quickly because of personal necessity. This seller is hoping that a buyer will come along to take the property off his or her hands. Again, enter the bargain hunter who has alerted brokers and others that he or she can offer financial solutions to people with personal difficulties.

Pitfalls When Dealing with Motivated Sellers

The new bargain hunter must be aware, however, that dealing with motivated sellers is not all a bed of roses. It's often much more complex than the two examples we have presented. Typically, there are three major problem areas.

The Unsolvable Management Problem

In our second example, Tilly was quickly able to solve the property's problem through disciplined management. However, some properties have problems that are too big to solve. These include cases where the property is in a slum and social conditions make good management impossible; where the property is in violation of some city building and safety code and would cost a small fortune to correct; where there is a tenant association that is uncooperative and makes effective management impossible; or where some other uncorrectable problem exists.

The Unsolvable Personal Problem

Sometimes the seller has a problem that can't be solved by a quick sale. In the first example, our owner might instead have desperately needed money for treatment of his illness. He might have wanted to sell his house to raise money, yet still may have wanted to stay there. In this situation the proper answer for him might have been to refinance, not sell, or do a reverse equity mortgage. With either the owner could get money out, yet keep the property. A knowledgeable bargain hunter should see this and point it out to the would-be seller.

Note: It's important not to take unfair advantage of sellers motivated by financial need. There's a moral imperative here. In addition there's a legal one because an overzealous bargain hunter who takes unfair advantage of a seller's personal condition (particularly when it involves illness, either mental or physical, or age) could be liable for a lawsuit, recision of the transaction, and penalties. The idea is to provide a real solution to a seller's problem, not to browbeat an unwilling and weak seller into accepting an undesirable offer.

The Unsalable Property

Be sure that the seller's property is salable. Some properties are overmortgaged. Sure, the seller desperately wants out, but that seller may have no equity or even a negative equity. There may be no solution that you can offer here.

TIP

Highly motivated sellers frequently offer bargain opportunities. Those bargain hunters who can take advantage of the opportunity are investors who can offer solutions and provide a mutually beneficial transaction.

22
Getting Brokers to Work for You

A lament that I've heard over and again is: "A broker won't find a bargain for me. If the broker stumbled across a bargain property, why he'd would surely buy it for himself!" Makes sense, right?

Wrong! If you think this statement makes sense, then you really don't understand most agents. In this chapter we're going to examine what motivates agents and how to get them to help you.

Why Do I Need the Help of Real Estate Brokers?

As a bargain hunter, you need all the help you can get to find good properties. That goes without saying. But above all, you need the aid of real estate agents. Agents work full time at locating properties. There are few bargain hunters who know the market as well as agents do. The truth is that in most cases agents are the ones who stumble across and then list most of the real bargains.

I have read books by those who advocate bypassing the agent. "Go directly to the source," some advocate. "Go to the seller. That way you can save the commission." It sounds good. But how many of us have the time, the fortitude, and the endurance to spend the better part of every day scouting real estate?

Agents offer a nationwide system already established for marketing real estate. Everyone in this country knows about brokers. Nearly everyone uses them at one time or another. To my way of thinking, trying to create your own system of locating property when such an efficient and widespread system is already in existence doesn't make sense.

Don't try to circumvent the broker. Get the broker to do your work for you. Put the established real estate marketing system to work for you. It won't cost you money. As we'll see, it will make you more money in the long run.

Understanding Real Estate Agents

Some bargain hunters see the broker as an adversary or at best as a competitor. That's the wrong way to look at it. Yes, the agent can be a competitor, but only if you make that agent one. You can just as easily appeal to another part of the agent that will motivate that person to be on your side and want to help you.

The motivating principle is the commission. Real estate agents make their living on commissions. Offer an agent a commission and that agent will do just about anything for you, including in most cases help you buy the bargain property that he or she was thinking of buying. Here's why.

The Real Estate Agency Business

Contrary to popular belief, real estate is a hard business and not particularly well-paying. The statistics I've seen indicate that most agents make less than $50,000 a year. A great many make less than $35,000. Very very few make more than $75,000. Although they may be dealing in properties worth hundreds of thousands of dollars, they themselves don't make much money.

For many of us, this seems hard to believe. After all, if an agent gets a 6 percent commission, for example, and sells a $200,000 property, there's $12,000 right there. It doesn't take many of those sales to add up to big income, does it?

Yes, it does!

Most sales are "cobrokered," which means that there are two real estate companies involved, one bringing in the seller and the other the buyer. In such cases the commission is often split in half. In addition, within a company, a salesperson may have made the deal. That means a further split between the buyer's and the seller's agent. That big fat $12,000 commission can suddenly turn into a piddling $3000 commission to each of four individuals.

If a salesperson makes one sale a month (which is considered pretty good in the business) and only makes $3000 per sale, that comes to only $36,000 a year. Hardly a royal salary. (Remember, out of that income the agent must also pay for heavy car usage and sometimes for advertising and phone expenses.) Of course, top salespeople command a much better split.

Hungry for Business

As a result most real estate agents are always hard-pressed for cash. Of course, the agents would indeed love to invest in real estate themselves. Their more urgent concern, however, is making commissions to survive.

Now enter the bargain hunter who's looking for some good opportunities in real estate. You've talked to the real estate agent, explaining just what you're looking for (I'll talk about how to get an agent to remember you in a few paragraphs), and one day the agent comes across a good piece of property. Will the agent buy it or call you?

My experience has been that the agent will almost always call you first. The thought of a cash commission almost always outweighs other considerations in the mind of the agent. Getting that commission is the goal. Remember, most agents are in the real estate business first and the investment business second.

Agents Who Invest

That's not to say that agents don't invest in real estate. They do, and as often as possible. But typically, they buy a property only when they find that they have no opportunity to sell it to someone else. A bargain property appears, and the agent tries to find a bargain hunter but can't. Now the agent is faced with losing out entirely (having another agent make the sale) or personally buying the property. In this case the agent will try to buy.

The problem, however, is that it isn't easy for an agent to invest. Agents need cash like everyone else. In addition lenders are always suspicious of agents who are buying property and usually require stiffer qualifications for financing.

The Agent Will Work for You

As a result and contrary to common belief, a real estate broker will work hard for a bargain hunter and will show you prime properties as they appear. This isn't theory. Other bargain hunters and I have seen it work in practice time and time again. Brokers will work hard to find you bargains. After all, their business is selling real estate to collect commissions. Yours is finding bargain properties and making a profit. The two businesses make a very nice blend.

The key, however, is to convince the brokers that you can indeed make them a commission. If you're the sort who hesitates in the face of an obvious bargain, if you don't have any money (or appear not to), or if it in any way appears as though you're going to cheat the brokers out of their commissions, forget it because they'll forget you.

How to Get a Loyal Agent

Brokers thrive on loyalty. They long for loyal buyers. Selling real estate is a highly competitive business, and brokers realize that there is nothing to prevent you from working for months with one person and then, after that person has found just the property you are looking for, buying through someone else. Any broker who's been in the business any length of time knows the problems of disloyalty intimately.

Therefore, when you first approach a real estate agent, the foremost question in that agent's mind is going to be: "If I work hard and find the right bargain, will this person buy from me?" I know an agent whose first questions when dealing with an investor are: "What's my competition? How many other agents are you going to be asking to find bargains?" The amount of effort she puts into the bargain hunter's search is directly commensurate with the number of other agents involved. If she's the only agent, she works hard. If she's one of a dozen, she doesn't work at all. Oh, if something turns up, she'll call after she's called all the other bargain hunters who are working more closely with her.

Therefore, any way you can convince the agent that you really are working with him or her alone will be to your advantage.

The Buyer's Agent Agreement

If you've already bought or sold property through a broker, then you've established a bond, and getting that broker to work for you in the future shouldn't be a problem. On the other hand, if you're new to it, it could be difficult. I suggest the following:

1. Map out a specific area: a neighborhood, a small town, or any other well-defined region.

2. Visit a dozen or so brokers in the area and determine which is the most active and most knowledgeable. (You'll be able to tell this after a while just by talking a few minutes with an agent. Many simply don't know the territory. Others know it intimately.)

3. Once you find a broker whose knowledge and abilities you trust, give that broker a buyer's agent agreement for the specified area for a specified period of time.

A buyer's agent agreement states that if you buy property within a specific area, you agree to buy it only through the named broker. It's like a listing, only instead of listing property, you're listing your intention to purchase. The agreement doesn't prevent you from buying property through another agent; it just means that you'd have to pay a commission to the broker with whom you listed if you bought elsewhere.

Once you've given the agent the buyer's agent agreement, that agent should feel a certain loyalty from you and for you. After all, you've committed yourself to buy through that agent.

Limiting the Agreement

It's important to understand, however, that real estate is a localized business. An agent who, for example, knows the south side of town like the palm of his hand may not know much about the east side.

Similarly, we all are prone to making errors. We might think that an agent is perfect for us, only to discover a month later that he's a turkey who never works.

Consequently, it is important to put at least two limitations on the buyer's agent agreement. The first limits the territory: The agreement only applies if you buy property within certain specific boundaries—the agent's home field. The second limits the time: If the agent hasn't found a property for you within, say, 30 days, then the agreement ends and you'll try another agent.

How to Keep Agents Loyal

Finally, having once found good agents, it's important to keep them loyal. You do this by paying them and not cheating them out of a commission.

The temptation here can be great. Sheila was the sort of bargain hunter who not only wanted a bargain but also wanted to be sure that she was the only one who profited from it.

Sheila signed a buyer's agent agreement with Tito, an agent. Within 3 weeks Tito produced a property. It had a market value of $150,000, but Tito could get it for Sheila for $120,000. She dove for it and the deal was made.

Worrying about the Commission

However, Sheila began thinking about that commission. Since Tito had both listed and sold the property, he was getting a full commission, in this case 7 percent, or $8400. She said to Tito, "This was too easy. You didn't have to work for the commission. You just called me up and I bought the property. You should give me at least half."

Tito was appalled. He thought of all those weeks and months he'd spent searching for properties. He remembered the times he'd been beaten out by other agents, been humiliated by buyers or sellers who bought elsewhere, and suffered long dry periods without sales. Immediately, his opinion of Sheila went down a notch. Nope, he said, he wouldn't split his commission.

Sheila saw that he was serious, so she considered. She was putting $10,000 down on the property. The seller would give most of that money to Tito as his commission. She had an idea.

Taking Advantage of the Broker

Sheila waited until the deal was ready to close. Then she announced that she'd had a financial turn of events. The money she'd had to make the deal was now committed elsewhere. She couldn't go through with it.

The seller was angered and threatened to sue both Sheila and Tito. Tito was mortified. What was Sheila thinking?

Then Sheila announced that she would make the sale if instead of putting $10,000 down, she only had to put $1500 down. The balance could be in the form of a third mortgage to the seller.

The seller thought it was great. That was just the amount he owed Tito. If Tito would take a third mortgage for $8500 for his commission instead of cash, the deal could still go through.

The ball was now in Tito's court. He could of course refuse. But then he would lose the sale altogether (since other agents were aware of the property and had offers ready to present if the deal fell through). In addition he might be named in a lawsuit by the seller. So Tito accepted. The third mortgage was written—no payments, no interest, and all due and payable in 5 years—and the seller transferred it to Tito.

As soon as the deal was closed, Sheila approached Tito. She said she was sorry that things had worked out the way they had, particularly since her finances had now cleared and she had some money. To help straighten things out, she would be willing to buy that third mortgage from Tito for cash for half its value.

Tito could wait 5 years to collect or take cash now. As anyone who knows the future value of money will tell you, it was no choice at all. Tito took it.

Sheila was all smiles. She got the property and half the commission. But Tito was no fool. He knew exactly how he had been played. Not only would he never give another bargain opportunity to Sheila, he would also see to it that as many other agents as possible knew about her and stayed away.

Yes, Sheila got her great bargain, but she probably lost out on many more bargains in the future.

The Moral

The moral here is simple: Don't bite the hand that feeds you. In a good deal, there's more than enough money to go around. Let the agents have their share and they'll come back later with more for you. Try to get more than your share and you can take yourself out of the market.

My Bias

Now that you've read this chapter, I'm sure you're wondering about my own bias. Does the chapter sound as if it's been written by an agent? If so, should what is being said here be taken with a grain of salt?

Yes, I hold a real estate broker's license and have done so for many years. However, I have not acted as an agent (listing or selling for others) for the last 25 years. In fact I didn't make any real money in real estate until I stopped working as an agent and became an investor for myself. To this day, whenever I buy or sell real estate, I always try to use an agent—and I always pay the commission.

23

Buying Mortgage Paper for Profit

This is a bargain hunting method that relatively few people have discovered; hence, it may be ripe for picking. It offers enormous potential rewards with usually manageable risks. It's an area, however, that requires two things to succeed: some expertise and some money.

In Chapter 3 we looked at profiting from a stage 1 opportunity by buying a property in foreclosure directly from an owner. Here we're also considering investing in a property that's in foreclosure, but this time getting it from a lender.

This may seem a strange place to find a bargain. Why are we concerned with the lender? Isn't the lender the one who's doing the foreclosing?

Yes, and for the lender it can be an experience almost as unpleasant as for the owner—and therein lies the opportunity. Consider this example.

The Reluctant Lender

Henry sells his home. The buyers get a new first mortgage, but they don't have enough for a full cash down payment. So Henry carries back some "paper"; he gives the buyers a second mortgage for some of his equity in the house. The payments are "interest only," meaning that the mortgage balance never gets any lower. Henry just gets paid the interest on it. It's all due and payable in 3 years. The deal looks like this:

Cash down payment	$10,000
Henry's second mortgage	$40,000
First mortgage	$150,000

The buyers pay for 3 years. However, at that time the second mortgage is due. The buyers now owe Henry his full $40,000 in cash. But the buyers don't pay.

The Stonewalling Borrowers

There are no more interest payments coming in, and the buyers don't return Henry's calls when he asks them when they are going to pay off the mortgage. Henry goes to see what the problem is. When he gets to his old house, he's told to get lost and the door is slammed in his face. The current owners won't pay and won't talk.

That second mortgage, which Henry took back at the time of the sale of his property, now looks like a real headache. He is owed the full $40,000, but how does he collect it? Should he foreclose?

What's worse, while he's trying to figure out what to do, he receives notice that the buyers have stopped making payments on the first mortgage as well. The bank, which holds the first, has just filed a notice of default. (Holders of secondary financing usually pay a nominal fee to a service set up at the time of sale that notifies them if the first is in default.) Henry goes to see the broker who handled the sale and is told that if the first forecloses, he could stand to lose all of his $40,000.

The Order of Foreclosure of Mortgages

To understand Henry's dilemma fully, we need to understand how mortgages are prioritized. As those familiar with real estate know, mortgages are numbered in order of their chronology. (This is an easy concept to grasp but absolutely vital.)

Let's say I loan you $100. You agree to pay me back. Now you go to another friend, André, and borrow $50. You also agree to pay André back.

Tomorrow you earn $100. Who do you pay back first? Do you pay me? Do you pay André? Or do you give a little to each of us?

In real estate these questions could never arise because we would all immediately know who gets paid back first. The rule is: In foreclosure the mortgage placed on the property first gets paid back first. That's why a first mortgage is called a "first," a second mortgage is a "second," and so forth. In a forced sale, whatever money is realized from the sale goes first to the first mortgage. Then and only then, if there is anything left, is the second paid, then the third, and so on down the line.

TIP

There is a method, called subordination, of keeping a loan in a secondary position even if it's chronologically placed first on a property, but that's not germane here; we examined subordination in Chapter 17.

Henry's Problem

In Henry's case he holds a second mortgage, and the first is foreclosing. If this process were to continue, at the time of the foreclosure sale the property would go to the highest bidder. Naturally, the holder of the first would bid the full amount of the first loan, in this case $150,000. If there were no other bids, the property would be sold to the holder of the first. Henry would get nothing.

Remember the priorities of mortgages: The first money realized goes to the first, and only then does anything left over go to the second and so forth. If only $150,000 were realized (bid by the holder of the first), there would be no money whatsoever left over. Henry's mortgage and any interest in the property would be wiped out.

Protecting the Secondary Lender's Interests

To protect his interests in the property at a foreclosure sale by the first, Henry therefore has to see that the first doesn't foreclose. The only good way to avoid this undesirable eventuality is to get the first mortgage out of foreclosure. To do this, Henry himself would need to quickly make up the back payments on the first mortgage out of his own pocket. Once the back payments (and penalties) on the first were made up, the default would be removed and the first would be out of foreclosure. (If Henry's second mortgage is written correctly, it will allow him in this situation to add all payments made on the first mortgage to the second.)

This only ends Henry's immediate problem. The long-term problem, what to do about getting paid on the second, remains. To settle that, he would then have to begin foreclosure on his second, all the while continuing to make up the payments on the first.

The reason Henry would need to foreclose on his second would be to get back his title to the property. Once he had title, he could try reselling, hoping to recoup his money.

Henry's Foreclosure Does Not Affect the First Mortgage

Note that if Henry forecloses on his second mortgage and the property goes to sale, the first mortgage is unaffected. Because of its superior position, the first continues to remain in force. Henry's foreclosure (assuming he is the only one to bid) allows him to gain title to the property and then, ideally, to resell, subject to the existing first of $150,000, in order to recoup his money.

It's important to be clear about this. If Henry forecloses and gets title to the property, he doesn't eliminate the first. It's still there. He simply secures his own position.

How's Henry Feeling?

Henry is not a bank, nor is he a mortgage banker or a mortgage broker. He's only a homeowner who carried back a second mortgage to facilitate the sale of his house. Now to save his money, it appears that he'll suddenly have to put forth additional money and use skills and knowledge he doesn't have. Henry's feeling uncertain, frustrated, and probably more than a little bit scared.

What Henry would like most of all right now is for someone to bail him out. That someone could be you. Let's consider the deal from a bargain hunter's viewpoint.

Is It a Bargain?

In the original sale, the buyers (the current owners) put down $10,000. It's been 3 years. Even with very slow appreciation, if we assume that the property has gone up only 2.5 percent a year, today it's worth about 8 percent more than when it was sold. It's gone from $200,000 to possibly $215,000:

Current owners' equity (includes
  $15,000 appreciation plus $2000
  equity return on first mortgage) $27,000

Henry's mortgage	40,000
First mortgage (it's gone down $2000 in 3 years)	148,000
Present worth	$215,000

Note what's happened over the 3 years. The first mortgage has been paid down a little. The house has gone up in value a little. This has turned the current owners' equity from $10,000 into $27,000.

But for one reason or another, the current owners don't care about this equity because they're allowing the property to sink into foreclosure. Similarly, Henry doesn't much care about this equity either. He wants to get out of the problem the easiest way possible. He wants to get rid of his headache. But the bargain hunter cares.

The Bargain Opportunity

As the bargain hunter, you can make Henry an offer. Henry already knows that if he forecloses, he's going to have to come up with payments and penalties on the first as well as the costs of foreclosing on the second. He also knows that he's going to be moving into foreign territory.

You can relieve Henry's anxiety. You can take away the pain, the frustration, and the work.

But first you must know what it's going to cost you. From the lender of the first you can find out the exact payments and penalties. From the trustee you can find out the exact costs of foreclosure sale. We'll assume here that these two costs come to $4000.

Once you know the exact costs, you can enter the picture, offering to take that troublesome second off Henry's hands (have it assigned to you). Henry is sure to like that idea. You, of course, remind him that there are costs and risks involved.

You can point out that Henry's second is now really worth $4000 less because that's the amount he'll have to put out in cash to protect it. Instead of a $40,000 second, in reality he only has a $36,000 second.

In addition there are the risks of foreclosing. The current owners might sue or declare bankruptcy or resort to some other tactic, any of which could slow down the foreclosure process. During the whole time the process is delayed, the payments on the first, plus the taxes and insurance on the property, will still have to be paid.

Even if the foreclosure is ultimately successful, there's the chance that the current owners might refuse to leave the property and might fight an eviction suit. This could delay things further.

All of these are in fact real risks.

You point out that you are willing to take on these risks as well as relieve Henry of the burden of the second. You make him two different offers.

Your Offers to Henry

First, you offer him $20,000 in cash. If Henry accepts, he signs the mortgage over to you, and he's permanently out of the picture.

Second, as an alternative, you offer to have him sign over the mortgage to you in exchange for a promissory note of $30,000 that bears no interest for 6 months. If by that time you are able to foreclose on the property and gain title (and evict the current owners), you'll exchange the promissory note for a fully assumable second mortgage in favor of Henry on the property for $30,000 at a low rate of interest, due and payable in 7 years.

If you can't complete foreclosure in 6 months, then you'll give Henry back his original second, provided he compensates you for any costs you've incurred. If at any time the current owners suddenly have a change of heart and make up the default on the second, you and Henry will split the receipts.

What Will Henry Do?

Both of these offers have appeal to Henry. If he takes your first offer, he gets out free and clear, with no more problem or headache. But instead of $40,000 (the face value of his second), he receives only $20,000. If he takes your second offer, he gets nothing immediately. But if you're successful, in 6 months he gets a second for $30,000 ($10,000 more than the cash offer).

The Benefits to You

Under the first offer, you have to put up some $20,000 for a short time to Henry and about $4000 to make good the first mortgage. However, you immediately get the rights to collect on the second. You file a notice of default and start foreclosure.

Once you gain title through foreclosure, you refinance the property. Assume it's worth $215,000 and you get a 90 percent loan, about $193,000. That's enough to recoup all the money you paid Henry and pay off the existing first mortgage of $148,000 plus any additional costs you have incurred on the deal. With no net investment, you've just acquired a 20 percent interest in a property with about half in cash!

Under the second offer, the same thing happens. However, you don't have to give Henry the $20,000 up front. Should there be problems and you can't clear the property, Henry is always there to bail you out after 6 months. But if everything goes well, you end up with the same property worth $215,000. With a $193,000 first mortgage plus an assumable $30,000 second (that is, you can sell the property to someone else, who then assumes the mortgage), you thus have cashed out about $40,000 for an expenditure of only $4000. Again, not a bad bargain.

Does It Really Work?

In principle, yes. The idea is that we find a private lender who is facing foreclosure on a second (or third) mortgage. We examine the property. If there is enough equity to warrant our interest, we make an offer.

Our example here tries to hit a middle ground. In the real world, you are likely to find properties that offer a much greater equity as well as some that offer less. The point is that by being willing to take on the foreclosure risk, you can cut yourself in for a handsome piece of the action.

Remember, a novice lender faced with a foreclosure that he or she doesn't want to get involved with is usually very interested in bailing out. Many such lenders will be extremely thankful to any person who offers to take the problem off their hands.

How Do I Find Lenders
Like Henry?

One last question remains: Where do we find people like Henry? We've already talked about the various methods of locating properties that are in default. We then went on to deal with the owner-borrower. In this chapter we are using the same methods. These not only give us the name of the owner-borrower but also that of the lender who is waging foreclosure. This time we just go see the lender.

Hidden Perils

I've already suggested some of these. Although it's unlikely, the borrower could fight back with lawsuits, bankruptcy, partial payments, or other devices to drag out the proceedings. The borrower could refuse to vacate the property.

(Note: If the borrower has a change of heart and suddenly pays up, the worst that's likely to happen is that we'll end up with a second for $40,000 for which we paid half. This can be resold to get out our cash and probably a 50 percent profit.)

Other potential problems: There could be other liens on the property that we haven't considered. There could be back taxes.

There's also the physical condition of the property. People who allow their homes to go to foreclosure don't usually keep up the yard or the house. There could be physical problems hidden in the property.

Or there could be something else wrong, including problems with the title itself.

Protecting against the Perils

Can we protect ourselves against these perils? Not entirely. We can get a preliminary title report from a title insurance company. This will probably (but not necessarily) reveal most defects, including other mortgages or liens. It can be a useful guide depending on how up-to-date it is.

We can try to make a deal with the borrower: "Move out next week and sign a deed to me and I'll give you $500 cash." If this works, we've avoided the problems of foreclosure and occupancy. (See Chapter 3 for the perils in making such offers.)

We can scrutinize the property and make a guesstimate of its condition. This could be more difficult if the borrower refuses to let us inside. Nevertheless, we can usually make a fairly good judgment. (We can also hire structural engineers, builders, etc. to help here.)

Recommendation

At the outset I said that this technique requires some money and some expertise. Yes, it is risky. But after you've done it awhile, as with anything else, you become pretty good at judging the risk.

For the person who has some money and time to invest, this could be a source of bargains. But be prepared to sustain some losses and incur some problems when you first tackle it. And it's a good idea to have a real estate attorney in reserve to handle any legal problems that arise.

24
Seven Real Estate Bargains to Consider

What makes one piece of property a bargain and not another? I've found that there are seven critical areas that must be considered every time we look for real estate bargains. It's important to understand that we're talking about investing, not about buying for our own residence; when we buy for ourselves, the considerations will surely be different.

Why must we examine these seven areas? The seven are those that I, and other investors I've talked with, have found to be vital. Taking these into consideration can lead to high profits. On the other hand, failure to consider any one of them could result in an investment disaster.

The seven areas to watch out for are:

1. *Price.* The property sells for substantially below market.
2. *Terms.* The down payment, interest rate, terms, or other conditions of financing are below market.
3. *Rental and resale market.* The property is mistakenly positioned in either of these markets.
4. *Location.* The location is actually better than the seller acknowledges.
5. *Condition.* It's a "distressed" property that you can fix up.
6. *Zoning.* The zoning provides an opportunity to put the property to a higher and better use.
7. *Occupancy.* It's vacant and there's no problem, or it's occupied, you can't get the tenant out, and this is a big problem.

If you're familiar with real estate transactions (or have read books on real estate investment), you've probably seen these seven mentioned in one or more contexts. I seriously doubt, however, that you've seen all of them listed together or placed in this priority.

Note, for example, that I have listed location as number 4. Yet all real estate agents and investors who know their salt have been taught that location is the prime factor in real estate. In fact the most important rule when buying real estate has always been location, location, location!

Not anymore! Especially not when we're looking for bargain property. Here location is but one of many factors; others, such as price, terms, and market, can be far more important.

To put it differently, when you first bargain hunt, you'll probably have to change many preconceived notions you may have about investing in property. I suggest that you carry a small piece of paper with the preceding list written on it. That way, each time you check out a piece of property, you can go down the list and be sure you haven't overlooked something important.

Understanding the Big Seven

To be a winner, a property must be outstanding in at least one of the first six areas. To avoid being a disaster, a property must have no negatives in any of the seven areas.

If this judgment seems arbitrary, rest assured that it isn't. I arrived at this list of seven after having gone through many cases, including some instances of bitter experience.

TIP

The property must be outstanding in at least one of the first six areas.

TRAP

The property should have no overwhelming problem in any of the seven areas.

For the remainder of this chapter, we are going to examine in detail each of the seven critical areas. We'll look at examples and learn how to recognize benefits as well as problems.

Price Bargain

Everyone recognizes a price bargain. It means that you're getting a piece of property at below market value. If comparable houses are going for $150,000 and you can buy one for $130,000, it would seem logical to say that as soon as you've made your purchase, you've acquired a $20,000 profit:

Market value	$150,000
Purchase price	130,000
Profit	$20,000

But it really isn't that simple. If you've had any experience in real estate, you quickly realize that there's usually a catch when the price is low. There is some problem that is causing the low price. It might turn out that the property requires expensive work and that $20,000 below market isn't enough of a price cut to make it worth buying. Or it may be that our game plan calls for a quick resale, yet the costs of resale will eat up the whole $20,000. Consequently, what may at first seem to be a profit could in reality be a loss.

The point is that just because the price is low doesn't necessarily make the property a bargain. We need to avoid "price fixation"; that is, we have to avoid thinking that just because it's below market, it's a good deal. Maybe it is, but then again maybe it isn't. Here are three problems to watch out for when determining whether a property priced below market value is truly a bargain:

1. Hidden problems with the property
2. Underestimated costs of liquidation
3. Invalid estimate of true market value

If none of these problems exists, you may have a terrific bargain on your hands. You may have gotten what everyone is looking for. On the other hand, if even one of the problems exists, watch out!

Let's take these one at a time.

Hidden Problems

P. T. Barnum is reported to have said, "There's a sucker born every minute." The question with regard to a house with a low price is: Who's the sucker? Is it the seller for selling low? Or is it us for buying without knowing why the seller is offering a low price?

TIP

Never buy for less than market price until you know exactly why the seller is willing to cut the price.

Here, along with their value to us, are the most common reasons a seller would be willing to take a lower price:

Why Seller Is Willing to Take a Low Price	*Value to Us on a Scale of 1 to 10*
1. The property is condemned.	0
2. The property will cost at least as much to fix up as the amount by which the seller is reducing the price.	0
3. The seller is desperate to sell.	10
4. The resale market is terrible right now.	5
5. The seller is stupid and doesn't know the property's true value (like finding a living dinosaur).	1
6. The property is in bad shape (but we know how to fix it up for next to nothing).	10
7. We don't know why.	−10

In other words there are usually only two and a half good reasons for a reduced price that are of benefit to us: The seller is desperate for a quick sale or the property is a fixer-upper that we know how to fix up better than the seller does or the market is so terrible that the seller has to cut the price and we can buy and hold for a long time (I don't recommend this). I did give 1 point for finding sellers who don't know the true value of their property; however, today almost all sellers have an inflated idea of their property's value, not the other way around.

If we find a property with any of the good reasons present, then we should consider buying. On the other hand, if the seller has one of the other reasons for selling lower or if we don't know the reason, then we should walk away from the deal.

Underestimated Costs of Liquidation

Assuming that we are indeed fortunate enough to buy a property for substantially below market price, have we then immediately made a profit?

Not necessarily. Remember, we don't actually make our money until we sell the property and receive our check. If our plan for the property consists of buying and then quickly reselling, the liquidation costs could eat up our potential profit. There's an old rule in real estate that any agent can vouch for: Don't count the money until it's in your pocket.

Consider our example: Given that the market value is $150,000 and we buy for $130,000, have we really made a $20,000 profit? Before we can pocket the $20,000, we will probably need to resell the house. (We talked about refinancing and cash out on purchase in Chapter 17.) While we can indeed do this on our own either as a for sale by owner (FSBO) or as a trade, in many cases we'll need the services of an agent to get a quick, clean sale, particularly if it's a tight market (we'll see other important reasons to use an agent as we go along). This means that we'll need to pay the agent a commission. There may also be closing costs, mortgage payments, and fix-up costs:

Commission	$9,000
Closing costs	3,000
Mortgage payments	2,000
Fix-up costs	1,000
Liquidation costs	$15,000

What should be obvious is that, when we subtract the $15,000 in potential costs involved in realizing that profit, we find we've only made about $5000 instead of a $20,000 profit. This $5000 isn't bad, but it's not quite the treasure we thought we'd get.

But it could have been if we'd gotten into the property at a lower price, say, $120,000 instead of $130,000. Buying for $30,000 less than market value makes it a real bargain. At that much less, after our roughly $15,000 in expenses we could still get a $15,000 profit.

Remember, just because a property is priced below market doesn't mean it's a good deal. It's the amount below market after liquidation costs that counts.

Invalid Estimate of True
Market Value

Finally, when we come across a surprisingly low price, we have to be sure that there really is value there. We have to be wary that maybe it might only be our interpretation of the price that's low. In other words do we really know what the true market value of the property is?

Market value is a wonderful term. It implies precision and knowledge. But in truth it's nothing more than an educated guess.

What is the true market value of any property? It's what a buyer is willing to pay for it. Without a buyer the property has no market value.

When you're looking for a price bargain, be sure that you estimate a property's market value on the basis of the best evidence. Go to a nearby real estate agent and ask to see "comparables" (comps), data on recent sales of similar properties. Most real estate agencies are computerized and can get this information for you in a matter of minutes. Get a comparative market analysis (CMA) that rates comps in the area.

Accurately estimating the true market value does take time and does require good judgment, but it's an essential part of bargain hunting.

To sum up, these are the three areas to watch out for when you are searching for a price bargain: A property can only be a bargain in terms of price when it has no hidden problems, when you've taken its liquidation costs into account, and when you know its true market value.

Terms Bargain

We've mentioned that many buyers and even more sellers are hung up on price. Their feeling is that the only thing that counts in real estate is the sales price. Nothing could be further from the truth (but try telling that to an adamant seller). Consequently, it is sometimes easier to give the seller the full price and instead insist on wonderful terms. I find it positively amazing how some sellers will agree to what are horrendous terms for them just as long as they get their price. This is called a "terms bargain," or "financing bargain," for the buyer.

How can a property be a bargain if we get good terms yet pay the full price? It's easy.

Coming to Terms

An investor I know recently found a financing bargain. Josh located a three-unit apartment building for which the seller was asking $200,000.

Josh determined that each unit was rented out for $675 per month. That brought in a gross income for the whole year of about $24,000.

Josh knew that the value of apartment buildings is directly dependent on the income. He used a rule-of-thumb method of calculating: He divided the gross income ($24,000) into the asking price ($200,000) and came up with a multiple of 8.3. The building was selling for 8.3 times its gross.

Josh had studied the comps and had discovered that a multiple of 8.3 was a bit high. Most other similar buildings sold for only 8 times their gross annual income, so he offered $160,000 for the building. The seller turned down the offer and refused to make a counteroffer. She wouldn't take a penny less than $200,000. She wanted her slightly inflated price.

When the Owner Won't Cut the Price

Did Josh give up and wash his hands of the deal because he couldn't get a good price? Did he immediately assume that there was no bargain here? Not at all.

He looked at the property to see if it could be a terms bargain. When he examined the financing, he found out that the owner had only a single first mortgage of $75,000 on the building. There was no other financing.

Giving Price and Demanding Terms

Josh then offered full price with a token down payment of $10,000. (In Chapters 18 and 19, we saw how to raise the cash we need to make deals like this.) His offer further specified that the seller would agree to carry back the balance in the form of a second mortgage at 4 (yes, 4) percent interest.

Down payment	$10,000
Second mortgage	$110,000
First mortgage	$75,000

Josh's total mortgage payments would be about $1500 per month.

The seller objected that 4 percent interest was way below market. But Josh pointed out that she was getting her full price. She finally agreed to sell.

Josh jumped for joy. He had gotten his terms bargain.

Where's the Bargain?

At first glance it might appear that there was no bargain here. After all, Josh had paid full price, which was slightly above market. Yet there was indeed a bargain. Here's how to figure it:

Monthly income from property	$2000
Mortgage payments	1500
Positive cashflow	$500

The property will pay for itself. The $500 positive cashflow after mortgages will probably pay most of the tax and insurance costs. By the time Josh takes deductions on his taxes, if he qualifies for them, he may even end up with some cash in his pocket from this rental property.

But the real bargain has to do with rent increases. Rents are increasing across the country. If rents go up 7 percent a year for this building (they're actually going up close to this rate in many parts of the country as of this writing), the property's gross annual income after 5 years would increase to about $38,000. Assuming roughly the same gross multiplier the seller used (8 times income), Josh's property would then be worth $304,000.

Old gross income	$24,000
New gross income	38,000
Increase	$14,000

Josh bought for $200,000. After 5 years he could probably sell for $304,000. Before liquidation costs he would therefore stand to gross $104,000 on his $10,000 investment.

But there's more. Remember, the rents went up but the mortgage payments remained constant. At the fifth year, the expenses remained $24,000. But by then the income had grown to $38,000. In the fifth year, Josh was pocketing $14,000.

Big Challenge, Big Profits

Josh only invested $10,000. He was making almost that amount in cashflow on the property by year 5 even before taking into account the profit on a sale. The big cashflow plus the potential sales profit make the property a terrific bargain, a terrific financing bargain!

It was all made possible by the terms. To get her price, the seller was willing to accept a below-market interest rate and a low down payment.

(Beware of seller's problems with "imputed" interest. Check with your tax consultant.)

A seller who's adamant about price often can't sell and becomes desperate. In such circumstances a terms bargain may be possible. Therefore, when we look for bargain real estate, we must get beyond worrying only about price bargains. The financing often creates bargains that are just as good.

Rental and Resale Market

Throughout the world of finance, knowledge means power and money, and the same holds true in bargain real estate. If you know more about the rental or resale market than the seller does, you may be able to use this information to get a bargain. I call these "market bargains." Here are two examples.

A Rental Market Bargain

You've found a six-unit building that is for sale at 10 times the gross annual rent. Each unit is rented out for $500 per month, making the sales price $360,000.

However, you notice that the owner hasn't been watching the rental market. He says that tenants in the area are very transient and that he thus keeps his rents competitive so that his building will always be fully occupied. He worries that if he raises the rents, he will see more vacancies.

However, because you've been analyzing the local rental market carefully, you know that clean units with air conditioning (which these apartments do not yet have) are today renting for $650 a month. Given the present scarcity and desirability of such units, you figure that you can keep the building full all the time, with your vacancy factor down to virtually zero.

Calculating Current Value

So you buy for $360,000, fix up the units, and add air conditioning. Over a year, as the old tenants depart, you rent to the new ones at $650. Assuming you're not in a rent control area, when all the units have been rented at the higher price, your total annual income has gone up. Remember, price is a factor of rental rates.

Monthly rent, six units @ $650	$3,900
Annual rent ($3,900 × 12)	46,800
Multiplier	× 10
Current value	468,000
Less purchase price	360,000
Gross profit	$108,000

Of course, there was the cost of the air conditioning and the fixing up. But if that came to even $1500 a unit, or $9000 total, you've still made a hefty profit of close to $100,000 before liquidation costs. Your profit was possible because you knew more about the rental market than did the seller.

Yes, owners frequently don't know the rental market they are in. Once again, it's inertia. They've been renting low for so long that they sometimes assume that it's the only price they can get.

When You Don't Really Know the Market

Of course, the opposite could be true. The seller could be a bit underhanded. To make the income look higher, he might have rented out the units for $600 to relatives and friends. If we were unsophisticated, we might think that since other apartments (those that were fixed up and had air conditioning) were renting for that amount, the rent was fair, and we might thus pay a price based on the $600 rent.

As soon as we bought, however, the friends and relatives could move out, and we could find ourselves unable to rerent for more than $500 unless we improved the units. This is a classic case of the seller pulling the wool over the buyer's eyes, and it happens countless times. Be wary of it. Be sure that you're the one who knows the rental market better than the seller does and not the other way round.

A Resale Market Bargain

You've found a two-bedroom house that's selling for $180,000, which the owner and you agree is the market value. You alone, however, know that the area is desperate for three-bedroom houses and that the same house with three bedrooms would bring $225,000. You have also seen similar houses in which the garage has been converted to a third bedroom and a carport has been added to replace the garage. You know that the total cost for such a conversion will be no more than $15,000.

You arrange to buy at a price of $189,000. You then convert for $15,000 and thus have a property worth $225,000. As a result your potential sales profit before liquidation costs is $30,000.

This is a bargain that comes about because you know the resale market.

Location Bargain

As I noted earlier, this used to be considered the single most critical factor when buying real estate. Every investor and agent quickly learned that the three rules of property were location, location, location!

This is certainly still true if we're buying for our own residence. But with bargain hunting, the three items just covered (price, terms, and market) can be more important. To see the truth of this, consider the following example.

A Bargain in a Poor Location

We find a house in good condition that is selling for $50,000 under market value, but it's in the worst neighborhood in town. Should we not buy it because of its poor location? Note that the price is $50,000 under market value. Presumably this market value already takes the neighborhood into account. In other words the house is selling for $50,000 less than comparable houses are selling for, even in this undesirable area.

Let's put it another way. A house in a highly desirable area might sell for $200,000, but in a very undesirable area it might sell for half. But if we can buy that house in the undesirable area for $25,000, should we pass it up because of its location? True, we might only be able to resell it for $100,000. But should we turn our noses up at a $75,000 profit because the location isn't a top one?

I hope you see the point. When we bargain hunt, location is a factor, but not the only nor the most important factor. Were we buying a house for ourselves to live in, then I would put location right up there at the top. But if we're bargain hunting, there are other considerations such as a price, terms, and market that, quite frankly, can be more important.

Negative Locations

There is a negative side to location, however, that we must also consider. Sometimes the location of a specific property is so negative that we will want to eliminate it from consideration. For example, the houses in a certain neighborhood may be selling for $150,000, and we find one there—the same model as the others—selling for $100,000. So it's a bargain, right?

Maybe not if the house happens to be one of the few in the tract that is right across the street from an undesirable element such as a factory. I saw this exact example not long ago. It was a tract of about 300 houses all in the price range mentioned. One end of the tract, however, bordered for only one block on an industrial area. Directly across the street from about six houses was a manufacturing plant. In addition to the factory-like setting (chain-link fence, weed-grown yard with greasy and broken machinery lying about, and workers parking cars on the street), the factory also exhausted noxious fumes, some of which drifted directly into the houses across the street.

Anywhere else in the tract, that $100,000 house might be worth $150,000, but when it was right in front of that factory, it really wasn't worth more than it was priced. In this case the location proved to be a significant negative factor.

Condition

When I talk about condition, I'm really talking about what is commonly called a "fixer-upper." Refer to Chapter 18 for the pluses and minuses of the field, how to find such homes, and how to price them.

For now, let's say that it's often possible to find a property whose price is less because of its distressed condition. If we're willing (either with our sweat or by hiring out the work) to buy at the low price and fix the property up, we can frequently make a profit.

Let's not consider properties priced just under their market value because of a slightly distressed condition. If all a house needs is paint and some carpeting, the seller may have subtracted the price of those items from the sales price. For example, the market value should be $125,000, but the house needs $3000 in painting and carpeting, so the seller has priced the house at $120,000. If we buy, we'll still have to spend the $3000, so in this case we might earn $2000 for our efforts. To my way of thinking, the effort just isn't worth the money, particularly when we consider the liquidation costs.

The really big profits come when the property is truly distressed. The house is slipping down a hillside and is condemned. Were it on sound footing, it would be worth $350,000, but because of its present condition it's going for $75,000. Can we buy it, somehow inexpensively fix it up, and sell it for a profit?

Or say that the property's market value should be $100,000, but the house's plumbing is corroded, its roof needs replacing, and it has to be replastered inside. It's selling for $50,000. Can we go in and do the work for next to nothing and reap a big profit?

Here the critical factor comes down to one thing. Is the physical problem with the house solvable or not? The rule is that, if we can't solve the problem, we shouldn't buy. But if we can solve the problem, we should seriously consider the property.

Zoning Bargain

Surprisingly, this is an area that most investors tend to ignore. Yet it's one that can frequently yield substantial profits from bargains.

In the first example in this book, I explained how a house turned out to be a bargain because it was on an R-2, or duplex zoned, lot. It was bought, split, and sold for a much higher price.

The same holds true for industrial and commercial property. In real estate it's called considering the highest and best use for property.

"Highest and best use" means that the owner is getting the most out of the land. If we have a lot zoned for three units and there is only a single house on it, it's not getting its highest and best use. If we have a lot zoned commercial and there's a three-unit residential building on it, it's not getting its highest and best use (which would probably be some sort of store). If it's zoned for office buildings and it only has a storage garage on it, it's not getting its highest and best use.

Underutilized Properties
Mean Bargains

Bargains can occur when we discover a property that is underutilized. Since the price is usually based on current utilization (with perhaps something thrown in for potential), we may be able to buy low, convert to a higher use, and resell high. In our example we bought a single-family residence and converted it to a duplex. By changing the property to a higher use, we increased the value and hence made our profit.

In most areas of the country, property built in the last 50 years has been constructed in accordance with its highest or best use. Developers have been keenly aware of costs and have built to get the most out of the land.

If it's zoned for three units and it's a recent structure, chances are that you'll find three units on it.

Look for Older Properties

But older property isn't always that way, particularly property built prior to or just after World War II. For some reason builders of that era frequently underutilized the lots, building single-family homes on multiple-zoned or commercial or even industrial property. In addition sometimes the zoning in an area has changed over the years, producing the same result.

What this means to us is a potential bonanza in zoning, particularly with older property. The key is spending the time to find underutilized property.

Watch Out for Midnight Conversions

Of course, many times others will have beat us to it. Current or former owners may have made "midnight conversions" (done without benefit of local building department approval). Garages, for instance, may have been converted to a second unit on a duplex lot. Beware of these.

This frequently happens in older areas or where the zoning has changed. But not always. Sometimes we can find property that has the right zoning and hasn't been converted. We can buy, convert, and take the profit.

Learn to Read the Zoning Maps

To do this, we need to know what the zoning is. The planning department of our city, county, township, or other government body has maps that pinpoint the zoning for every property in our area. These are often huge, cumbersome maps. But they are available to the public, and we can make copies.

In addition publishing companies that print city maps often print ones that include zoning references. These can usually be purchased at local stationery stores. Sometimes real estate boards will offer them to the public (either directly or through member brokers) as a service.

I always try to carry a zoning map when I go out scouting for bargains. A knowledge of the zoning could make a difference in finding a real treasure.

Watch Out for Zoning Errors

There is, unfortunately, a negative side to zoning. Sometime the maps are wrong and sometimes property owners are wrong in their knowledge of their land's zoning. If we buy a property thinking that it's R-2, only to find that it's really R-1, we could be in for a big loss.

I recently avoided such a problem by carefully checking with the city. I was looking at a property that was 50 feet wide by 250 feet long. It had a house on the front and two small potential rental units behind. The property was zoned R-3, meaning in this case that it could be used for up to three units, yet it was only being used for one. As a single-unit lot, its asking price was $155,000. However, as a multiple lot with three units rented out (converting the guest houses to rentals), it could be worth $100,000 more. My map clearly showed that it was R-3. Had I found a bargain?

Experience has taught me prudence. I went to the zoning department and rechecked on their enlarged maps. Yes, the first 20 feet of the lot were indeed zoned R-3. However, everything in back of the first 20 feet was zoned R-1. The lot had two zones on it and was totally unsuitable for more than one dwelling. Had I purchased hoping to take advantage of a higher use, I would have found my hopes dashed.

Zoning is a double-edged sword. If you're going to play the zoning game, be sure you know exactly what you're getting into. Yes, you can get real bargains here. But the unwary can also get hurt.

TRAP

Zoning should be a consideration anytime you look at bargain property. Be sure there isn't a big negative in the zoning that overwhelms the property's other positives.

Occupancy Bargain

This is like a veto. Occupancy doesn't usually add to the allure of a bargain property, but if it's going to be a problem, it can be a good reason to avoid the real estate.

Regardless of what our game plan for a property may be, we will almost always want to rent the property out. Rental income to offset mortgage and other expenses is a must in investment real estate. The question is: Can we rent it out? Or is there someone occupying the property who won't get out and who won't pay rent?

At first glance this may appear to be nothing more than a minor problem. There are eviction laws ("unlawful detainer") in all states; they come first on court dockets, they are relatively inexpensive to promote, and they work fairly fast. So what's the problem? If a tenant won't pay and won't get out, we evict.

It's not that simple. There are three possible problems with occupancy.

1. We can't evict tenants because they are protected by rent control laws. (The tenants could claim that we're evicting so we can raise the rent—and we could be subject to a lengthy court case and, if we lose, to severe penalties.)

2. The occupants say they have an ownership claim on the property and defend it in court. The court action is lengthy.

3. The occupants are ill or pregnant and claim that they can't be moved without sustaining physical injury.

If you haven't run into these problems on your own, rest assured that others have. The first and third listed here are fairly obvious, but let's consider the second.

When the Occupant Cries "Fraud!"

We buy a house at a foreclosure sale. It's a real bargain—we get it for half of its market value. However, the former owner is still occupying the property. She says there was fraud in the foreclosure and refuses to move out.

We know that the claim of fraud is ridiculous, so we start an unlawful detainer action to have her evicted. Normally, this takes only a month or so. And normally, the defendant in an unlawful detainer eviction doesn't show up, but in this case our former owner does appear. She claims that she was tricked into signing the former mortgage—that there was fraud—and the property should rightfully still be hers.

Fraud? Trickery? No judge is going to dismiss such charges out of hand. The case is held over. Now the legal battle begins. She hires an attorney, who takes depositions, makes motions, demands a jury trial, and moves the case from one court to another.

Note that we're not saying the former owner has a legitimate case. She only has the desire not to leave the property. She stays there, not paying us rent.

Weeks drag on into months as our attorney fees go up. In the case I'm thinking of, the investor ultimately spent $30,000 in legal and court costs, and it took 9 months to remove the former owner from the property. During that time, the investor's money was tied up in the house and he didn't get a penny of rent. He says the only reason he finally prevailed was because she ran out of money to keep paying her own attorney.

Occupancy Can Veto an Otherwise Good Bargain

It can happen. Occupancy can become a critical issue in the purchase of bargain real estate.

Therefore, whenever I consider purchasing a property, I always check to see if it's occupied, if the tenants are paying rent, and if they will move when I want them to.

The easiest way to handle this is to demand as a condition of purchase that the property be vacant at the close of escrow (time of sale). There should be no evidence (furnishings, clothing, or anything else) of any occupant in the property. Even if this means displacing a paying tenant, sometimes it's the safest thing to do.

On the other hand, sometimes you can't get occupancy for one reason or another. (In our example of a foreclosure, we as the buyer have no control over occupancy until we get title to the property.) In these cases we have to go on what we can see and use our best judgment.

That's why I list occupancy as a veto factor. If there's a problem here, it could be a reason to forget a would-be bargain that might otherwise have all kinds of advantages.

Putting It All Together

These, then, are seven bargain areas to be aware of. Remember, there's more than just price, and location isn't everything in this kind of property. Each item must be considered.

Appendix
Mortgage Priority in Foreclosure

It's important to know the priority of mortgages involved in foreclosure, particularly when bidding at a foreclosure auction (see Chapter 12). Here, briefly, are the rules:

1. The mortgage recorded first has first priority (is superior).
2. Mortgages recorded later have lower priority (are junior).
3. Any mortgage can foreclose (first, second, third, etc.), but such foreclosure will not affect superior mortgages.

The best way to be sure that we're clear on this is to take an example. Tracy's house has three mortgages on it:

Third mortgage	$10,000
Second mortgage	$20,000
First mortgage	$70,000

Case 1. The first mortgage forecloses. Tracy's house brings $100,000 at the sale.

In this case the loan with the highest priority (the first for $70,000) gets paid off with the first money. Then the loan with the next priority (the second for $20,000) gets paid off. Finally, the loan with the least priority (the third for $10,000) gets paid off. There's no money left, so the owner-borrower gets nothing.

Case 2. As before, the first mortgage forecloses. Tracy's house brings $75,000 at the sale.

Here the loan with the highest priority (the first for $70,000) still gets paid with the first money. Then the loan with the next priority (the second for $20,000) is paid. However, there is only $5000 left after paying off the first; therefore, the second only gets $5000 despite the fact that the mortgage amount is for $20,000. Since there's no money left after this, the holder of the third receives nothing.

Case 3. The third mortgage forecloses; the first and second are current. The sale brings $10,000. Here the holder of the third mortgage gets the whole $10,000. The first and second mortgages, which were current, are unaffected. The successful buyer now has title to a piece of property with existing first and second mortgages on it. True, this buyer paid $10,000; however, there are already $90,000 of mortgages still on it.

Index

About the Author

Robert Irwin, one of America's leading experts in all areas of real estate, is the author of more than 20 books, including McGraw-Hill's best-selling Tips and Traps series. For more real estate tips and traps, go to www.robertirwin.com.

SOUTHEASTERN COMMUNITY COLLEGE LIBRARY

3 3255 00066 7882

SOUTHEASTERN COMMUNITY
COLLEGE LIBRARY
WHITEVILLE, NC 28472